London to Ista...

Eye2i

Paul Sorensen

APS BOOKS
STOURBRIDGE

APS Books,
4 Oakleigh Road,
Stourbridge,
West Midlands,
DY8 2JX

APS Books is a subsidiary of
the APS Publications imprint

www.andrewsparke.com

Paul Sorensen has asserted his right to be identified as the author of this work in accordance with the Copyright Designs and Patents Act 1988

Map courtesy Dave Chisholm (www.davechisholmcartoons.com)

First published worldwide by APS Books in 2020

A catalogue record for this book is available from the British Library

ISBN 978-1-78996-207-9

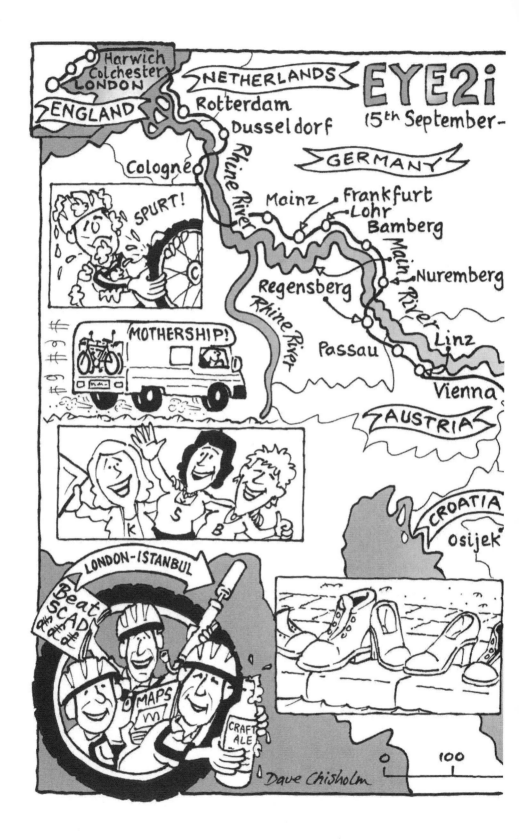

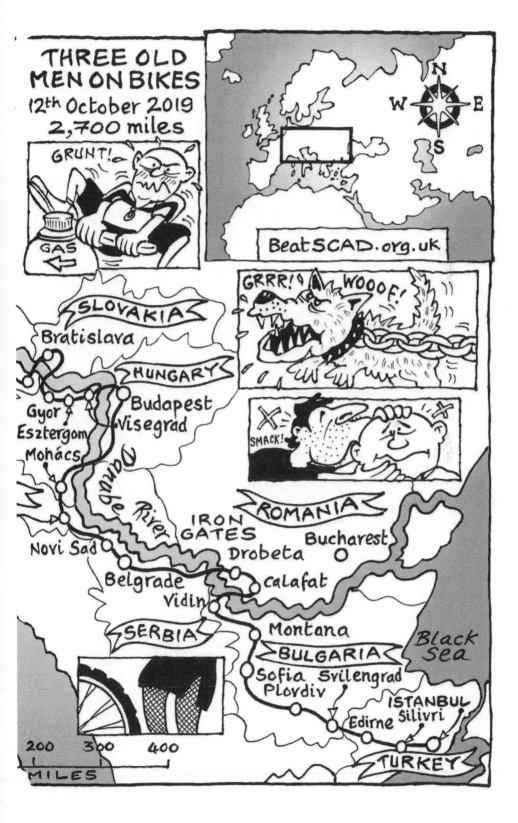

PREFACE

When three old men with ages totalling in excess of two hundred years decide to ride pushbikes from London to Istanbul, you might imagine that the machinery under their pudgy, near-septuagenarian backsides would be wheels to make Bradley Wiggins envious. Hmm...

In the shadow of the London Eye on September 15th 2019 the metal line-up was as follows: Clive was on a Globe bought from his daughter Amy's ex-boyfriend in 2011, Chris bestrode a Halfords special, a four year old Boardman, one up from the basic while mine was the basic, a Carrera, bought the week before the ride by my kids who were afraid that my old Apollo (also a Halfords basic) wouldn't get me out of London, never mind across Europe. All sturdy hybrids - gentlemen's tourers really. Total cost for three machines? £1000.

The campervan which was to be our refuge, our home from home for a month, was of an older vintage. Born in 2000 and soon to be dubbed the Mothership, the Peugeot Boxer Whirlwind Equipe, 1.9 Diesel, bore little resemblance to its dashing moniker. A double bed space above the driving cab was more claustrophobic than an overcrowded lift. The *lounge* area converted into a cosy double by wedging a ladder of struts across the aisle and slamming seats and cushions down to fashion a lumpy Slumberland. Clive took owner's prerogative and opted to kip aloft, leaving Chris and me to squabble over who slept nearest the toilet. Chris begged the weaker prostate but at our age, none of us could claim pee-free nights.

Clive's access to his crow's nest had been planned to be via a wooden ladder which would hook to the bed and rest on the floor but with the bed erected below this was going to be tricky. Clive researched an alternative and found a natty rope ladder which would hang straight down and not bother the boys beneath. Little did he know that scaling and descending this tricky blighter would have tested Sherpa Tensing, never mind the sixty-eight year old paunchy Rockell. With Paul lying beneath, Clive's night-time clambering in his sagging boxers was an unpleasant sight from my vantage point. He had to straddle my stock-still body on his vertical journeys. Despite this and other drawbacks which will feature during the saga, the Mothership fulfilled our needs and was to be the solid and welcome sign of home when one of us

1

reached the end of a sweaty stint and needed a cuppa, a snack and a pee.

The bike rack protruded from the rear of the Mothership and took all three machines - just. Every day of our journey we chained the bikes in a different order, thinking that we had found the best configuration. We never did - and when we thought we had cracked it, we promptly forgot how we had done it. And unless something is written down, we shall soon forget how this odyssey started...and how it ended.

PART I

BEFORE

1
WHO ARE WE?

Clive Rockell is a maverick character. Busy but laid-back, mild mannered yet argumentative; mercurial and dogged. A lifelong teacher and head of several primary schools - one of which he ran twice, his career was defined by itchy feet. If Clive stayed in a job more than three years he was letting too much grass grow. "I really should have been a project manager," he says now. In retirement he and his much more remarkable wife, Karen, (more of her later), moved from Glastonbury to Northampton, Karen to be close to family, Clive to hide himself away and plan ridiculous adventures. Bald and pot-bellied, he was once a fine sportsman. Now a dogged belief that optimism can overcome physical deterioration plagues him.

Clive must take the blame for the idea, much of the planning and certainly the drive to see this silly challenge through. For the record a Chelsea fan and long distance, Kingstonian F.C. fanatic.

Chris Dowdeswell is less maverick, better organised and pretty fit, despite a lifelong admiration of real and craft ales. His fitness owes more to being married to Sarah, a lifestyle guru and masseuse, than any particular initiative on his part. They spin together. Chris is thoughtful, makes lists, asks tricky questions; invariably wants a taster of beer before buying an unfamiliar pint. You know the sort. Annoying.

Chris was a banker, although his mates use a variant on the word. In semi-retirement now, he and Sarah moved house and did a huge renovation job while training for and doing the ride. Organised. Spurs season ticket-holder.

I, Paul Sorensen, was the weakest of the three in terms of input. My main contribution was to say *Yes* to Clive's ridiculous plan, without thinking. I'm a retired teacher who fancied a jolly - well perhaps a challenge. I'm quite calm (so are the others); I like a beer (so do the others); I have less of a belly than Clive, I don't like cycling very much, but I do like the craic after a long day in the saddle. I taught teenagers and try to keep that youthful mindset as I stagger into my dotage. I enjoy the freedom of self-determination each day, under some gentle guidance from my lovely partner Belinda. I am an unapologetic southern Man United supporter.

We three boys were at school together. Kingston Grammar School was an interesting mixed bag of a place in the 1960s. An all-boys, south London direct grant grammar, it was a school where kids came from a variety of backgrounds to be taught both well and indifferently, while the sexual and social revolution exploded around us. Our teachers were a combination of exhausted veterans, war-trained incompetents, inspirational tutors and newly-minted young professionals. What brought the three of us together, along with many others, was sport. The school was good at it. Friendships were made.

Hop on a few years and a group of us, led by Chris (*aka* Skipper) started an annual reunion long weekend break on a narrowboat. This still goes on every year with a group of eight or so, crammed into a boat which is entirely inappropriate for a bunch of seventy year olds who retain the mad ambition to drink two hundred pints of ale between them over the weekend. The Covid lockdown has prevented this year's excursion on the Kennet and Avon Canal but it was on one such jaunt, on the Grand Union Canal in 2009, that the glint appeared in Clive's eye.

The boys were tucking into a number of pints. Clive bided his time and then, as he reported in his blog, he pressed the start button. Here is how he remembers it, from his blog, The Diary of a Rockell-Powered OAP.

It was in the pub garden of The Sun in Nether Heyford, a decade ago, that three friends - fuelled by several pints - spoke about cycling projects. "Well Clive, you've done the 'Lejog - End to End' and we've all done London - Paris; what's next?" I don't know who asked but I can remember my reply.

"You know what I've always fancied a cycle across Europe and into Asia. I think we could do it." We were in our fifties and, given that we're not really cyclists, it was highly, highly questionable whether we could do it. That's the danger of drinking - an elevated assessment of your abilities, socially, physically and chronologically. 2,500+ miles equals a very high number of revolutions of a set of pedals - too high!

And yet, ten years later I've come up with a formula which might just work - fuelled not by pints but by the purchase of an old motorhome - a relay with each of us doing just over 800 miles @ 40 miles a day each (120 miles each day in total), from The London Eye to Istanbul. Simples!

On 15th September 2019, we shall set off after one revolution of the Eye into the eye of a cycling storm which will take us via Harwich, Hook of Holland, the rivers Rhine and Danube, down through Bulgaria and into Turkey to reach Istanbul and Asia within a month.

Currently, with just over 4 months to go, the emphasis is on planning, training and convincing ourselves that 25 (more or less) consecutive days of 40 miles of cycling each is do-able. And our aggregate age of 202 must provide us with the opportunity of breaking some Guinness World Record - it should do after all the money we've invested in that company and others like it for many, many years!

2
EDGING TOWARDS COMMITMENT
October 2017

Having identified two other old gits who were stupid enough to humour his adventurous whim, Clive set about pinning us down. As usual, I remained casual and unconcerned. Chris was still tentative given that he and Sarah had only just bought the wreck of a house that they intended spending their life savings turning into a super-home. But if we were going to do this thing, Chris wanted it done well. He and Sarah needed to approach both house renovation and cycling to Asia with the same intense focus.

In the October of 2017 we all got pissed at our biennial Scorpions lunch. The Scorpions were the former Sunday hockey side of the Old Kingstonians' Hockey club. In the modern world of Astroturf hockey the Sunday XI had folded many years earlier but a large bunch of ageing piss-heads still met at the Victorian hunting lodge in Bushey Park, Kingston, that was once the hockey home of past pupils. Simple fare: beer, curry, music, memory lane. Taxis home inebriated.

On this occasion Clive, in his cups, started pressing the commitment pedal and wouldn't let it drop. Clive's ability to sound very reasonable and unconcerned whether we went ahead with his barmy idea, whilst being hell-bent on ensnaring his prey, was evident. Chris's body language told a certain story beyond the genial, inebriate leaning against the bar with mouth sometimes missing pint glass. He had just flogged the family home in Witley and had bought a large bungalow which the estate agents had categorised as *needing some modernisation*. As he and Sarah waited for the deal to go through they decamped to tolerant friends, Maggie and Tony, for a modest two months. Chris was planning, initially, to erect a consulting studio for Sarah in the garden (posh shed really) at their new wreck in Hindhead, which would serve as their pied-a-terre when the wrecking ball started to demolish the rear half of their new bungalow. Bankruptcy featured somewhere in his thinking.

Chris recalls Clive gnawing away at his bone of ambition a month later. Clive produced an outline for us to salivate over. Initially he had conjured the insane notion of cycling from the westernmost part of Europe - say Lisbon - to the far east of the continent and, of course, into Asia. Well that got binned pretty quickly as suicidal. Little did we know that Croatian, Romanian and Bulgarian roads were to equally test our collective desire to stay alive in the not so distant future.

Chris quickly snuffed the out flame of imminent departure by simply saying, *no.*

Clive's selective hearing operated perfectly. When Chris said *no*, Clive was certain that he heard *yes* and proceeded accordingly. Of course 2018 was too soon. Chris's timing was quite right; 2019 was preferable, of course. Perhaps we could fit in a short trip across Cumbria and the Pennines in 2018 - coast to coast - as a warm up? After all, Chris and Sarah would need a break from all that planning and builders' dust.

As I say, Clive was a dog who couldn't be parted from his bone.

3
COAST TO COAST
April 2018

I may have given the impression that we were all novices at this cycling game. This is not true although we each shudder at the prospect of stretch lycra and lunchbox exposure. Chris and Sarah have done a fair amount of pedalling in the English countryside, usually fuelled by pub B+Bs, real ale and gin. Clive and Karen were not quite the regulars but Clive can boast a tandem ride with son George from Land's End to John O'Groats. Impressive eh? Indeed back in the mists of time in 2008, Clive (of course) had organised a London-Paris bike ride for a select group of a dozen or so, including our WAGs. The weather had smiled on us (apart from a God awful day crossing the South Downs to Newhaven) and we had made the two hundred miles or so without too much trouble. A decade later, a decade older, the trans-European project was of a different order altogether.

Clive's interim coast to coast plan found some favour with us all and a motley group of friends and relatives bought into the Whitehaven to Tynemouth jaunt across from the Atlantic to the North Sea. Clive had done a dry (I doubt it) run on his own (madness) and conveniently forgot to describe the steepness of gradients and the kamikaze downhills in his email briefings. Clive remembered that Spring 2018 adventure and how it helped shape the bigger challenge to come.

Looking back, with what was a very testing ride across the Pennines over four days, it was a very useful exercise. With Paul recovering from shingles, me recovering from general sloth and Chris looking a good climber, the value of proper training for such an activity became crystal clear. I certainly reflected that I was never again going to try something like this without proper physical preparation. I struggled badly and as organiser, felt a bit inadequate

Looking ahead to a prospective Eye to I, Internet searches found a variety of people, as strange as us, who had undertaken a similar trip. An interesting one was Helen Moat who followed the river idea all the way to the Black Sea and on to Istanbul from there.

Her fine book, A Time of Birds, tells the story. We were aware that the month we had allocated was just about all that we wanted and - in Chris' case, with a business and half-renovated bungalow to look after - could spare. Purchases of Cicerone guidebooks proved to be an absolute godsend in terms of planning even though 'The Rhine Cycle Route' was written out in the direction of Switzerland to Holland rather than, as we were travelling, the other way around. So, with a certain level of mental gymnastics, I worked on the route planning using the books and the clear - and as it proved accurate - distances in the books' appendices.

The banner picture on our Eye to I website has the three of us with our partners and cycling buddies, dipping wheels in the North Sea at Tynemouth. Despite the gradients, we had survived well enough for Clive's plan to become more than a dream.

4
SCAD AND THE GIRLS

I should pause here to introduce the girls. Belinda, my partner is a wonderfully supportive woman despite thinking that I had a screw loose when I threw my lot in with Clive's idea, without much thought. My reasoning was sound. Say yes now, think about it later. Belinda tends to engage brain earlier. She is another retired teacher who has lived in France and Spain and stayed pretty fit by way of aqua aerobics, ballet and tap. Gardening, walking, horse riding and volunteer work at a disabled riding centre complete the activity package. Cycling is a side-line but hooves come before wheels in her list of priorities. Having said that, she managed the Paris ride of 2008 and the short jaunt from Surrey to Somerset - or The Witley to Wells Wander - in 2010. Famously, on that trip, she cycled unerringly into the Kennet and Avon canal, somewhere near Newbury. Naturally I remind her of this as regularly as self-preservation allows.

For fifteen years we have cohabited in two places, Cheam in South London and Hawkhurst in deepest Kent. We'll get to one location soon; we just need a little more time.

Belinda is a doer. She recognised my need for challenge. As a professional I was good at completing things that I started; as a retiree I am a side-tracker; completion is manyana. Belinda knew that I needed to commit, needed a project. She may have reckoned without the whirlwind that is Sarah Dowdeswell, however.

As planning progressed the idea of the girls meeting us roughly halfway for R and R took shape. Vienna was identified as a great city break stop. Sarah took this a stage further by suggesting that the WAGs hire bikes and get in on the action. After all it is only 40 or 50 miles to Bratislava from Vienna and then only another 170 or so on to Budapest with breaks in Gyor and Visegrad.

In Belinda's house in leafy Cheam the prospect of a mid-European bike challenge made her blanch somewhat. "I don't think Sarah will manage to hire bikes that you can take across borders," she asserted confidently. Little did we realise that Sarah wasn't going to let a little thing like bike hire get in her way. Of course she found some trans-national cycling outfit which would allow us to pick up a machine in Vienna and deliver it to Budapest. Further, she hit Booking.com and other suitable sites to check us all into hotels in Vienna, Bratislava, Gyor, Visegrad and Budapest. The girls worked out that, if they rode with partners for say 20 miles at a stretch, the whole experience would be easy-peasy. And so it proved of course.

Sarah had been watching her husband wrestle with the equation:

Building Renovation + Cycling 2500 miles across Europe = Madness

And yet Sarah has a gung-ho gene which allows for eccentric behaviour when caution might be the prudent choice. Another phrase for gung-ho might be *Oh fuck it, just go for it.* In this spirit Sarah, by now treating her clients in a tiny room at the back of a ladies' hairdresser in Milford, planned for both building chaos and the Eye to I adventure.

Karen Rockell makes up this quirky yet stalwart female triumvirate. What Karen hasn't experienced in life isn't worth writing home about. She suffered for a decade with an unpleasant condition, *Auto-Immune Hepatitis.* This attack on her liver eventually gave her cirrhosis and a cancerous tumour which necessitated immediate transplantation. Following eight 120 mph journeys from their Somerset home to King's College Hospital, East London, with each journey leading to an aborted transplant operation, eventually it happened, in October 2010. So, despite never having taken a drop of the hard stuff, her failing liver was replaced by one which is proving an excellent replacement. When you ask her about this, she always looks wistfully into space and remembers the donor, a forty-five year old man, and his family's wonderful gift. Of course she now faces a lifetime of immuno-supressants and other drugs, along with a gluten free diet. Further, she has suffered from a SCAD - Spontaneous Coronary Artery Dissection. A SCAD is an unpredictable heart attack which affects otherwise healthy women. Only a limited amount of research has gone into the condition but Karen remains on a mission to remedy that.

Her recovery story is remarkable. Multiple gold medallist at both national and world transplants games, between 2011 and 2019, she lives each day as a blessing. Under lockdown now, in the Covid-19 summer of 2020, she is one of the most vulnerable but little seems to faze this brave and resolute woman.

Back in the summer of 2008, when we pedalled to Paris, a number of the group raised money for the British Liver Trust. Karen wasn't well enough at the time to make the trip, although she flew to celebrate with us in Paris. Chris and Sarah cycled to raise money for the Surrey Air Ambulance. Tragically Sarah's brother had died in a road accident in Dorking in April of that year. They felt that by riding in support of the air ambulance crew who had tried so valiantly to save Simon, they would honour his memory. And they did. As we neared Paris, Chris and Sarah had a poignant remembrance photo taken in Gouvieux, a town twinned with Dorking.

For all the joy and excitement of the adventures that we planned, each of us has a back story that includes sadnesses, indeed tragedies. Joy and celebration too. We have wonderfully supportive families and friends, children and grandchildren. As we were planning and executing our adventure the grandchild production line was in full swing. Three babies were born in the run-up. Rex, Jacobi and Finley were added to the burgeoning list of small fry swelling the three families.

Raising money for a good cause was not a driving force. The challenge was enough. As time moved on, though, Clive posed the question. As usual his line was, *if you want to support your own charities or none, it's entirely up to you...but I'm going to try to raise a little for BeatSCAD*. Now Chris and I have an aversion to touting a tatty piece of paper round pub tables press-ganging mates into parting with tenners or twenties which they had earmarked for the next round. However we felt that as rebels without a cause, supporting just one worthwhile charity - *BeatSCAD* - was a great idea. As long as persuasion was low-key, via a Just Giving site, so we didn't have to tout lists around...

Chris and I took the trouble to find out just what we were promoting - and just how little money, and therefore research, has gone into this frightening heart problem. Clive set a target of £1000. Well, as time would tell, we were to blow that out of the water.

5
CLOSING IN ON COMMITMENT:
TALES OF A BULGARIAN RECCE

To forestall the Dowdeswells using their building site of a home as an excuse for further hesitation, Clive and I set out, in October 2018, to reconnoitre the chunk of our route which has no established cycle route. The *Eurovelo 6* can take you from the Atlantic coast of France to the Black Sea. Clive had worked out that we could bike down through the Netherlands (*Eurovelo 15*), pick up the Rhine, the river Main and the Danube, following the *Eurovelo 6* much of the way. The only catch was the need to turn south in Romania and head down through Bulgaria on roads not particularly suited to bikes. The Bulgarians don't cycle much and don't give too much of a monkeys about cycle lanes. The Turks don't do two wheels either. Clive and I thought that Chris might be nervous of Bulgarian heavy goods vehicle drivers thundering past aged Brits wobbling along through the Balkans. Well, who wouldn't be nervous?

Clive had booked *Vueling* (no I hadn't heard of them either) for the hop to Sofia from Luton. We almost missed the plane as we somehow lost our sense of direction outside the airport and had to scurry over fences and through a multi-storey car park before going through an odd door to the terminal. The security queues resembled post lockdown IKEA lengths before a man with an impressive identity lanyard spotted our distress and hurried us through as if we were VIPs. Perfect. If we couldn't organise ourselves for a simple short haul flight, what chance did we have of getting across Europe under pedal power?

Very soon we were in a very different part of Europe.

***

Terminal 1 at Sofia was a distinctly budget unit - rather like the cramped hangars which greet you on arrival at an outpost of empire or a small Greek island. Little did we know that Terminal 2, a glossy, EU-sponsored erection, was a stone's throw away.

Documentation to take a hire car across the Turkish border would take a week but we could use it in Bulgaria. Clive recognised a flaw in his research and for a moment looked devastated - but then quickly adopted his more usual, *Oh well, we'll just have to make the best of it* face. I tried to maintain a quietly supportive demeanour whilst privately thinking *Oh, FFS I leave you to do all the work and you let me down.* We didn't have that long and so we headed out of the capital on Route 8 and were soon in pothole territory. We think that we have pot-hole problems. The Bulgarians have pot-craters more like. Jesus! Beyond the few urban areas, rural Bulgaria doesn't seem to have seen much EU cash injection in the decade since the Bulgars threw their lot in with Merkel. Poor peasant life is the norm and few, if any, spoke English though, to be fair, why would they?. Our charades expertise came in handy. Luckily beer is beer in any language. The Cyrillic alphabet is suspended for Stella or Heineken.

***

We got ourselves lost as we were slaloming the craters. Google maps took us along remote tracks where chained dogs barked and local workers stared quizzically. After an hour or more we found our way back to Sofia and started again. Easier said than done since Sofia in Cyrillic begins with a C and ends with mirrored N and R. If I could press the right keys now I'd show you. Such is my level of incompetence. As for our journey to the Turkish border via Plovdiv, guesswork and blind faith in our sense of direction would have to see us through. The auguries were not good.

We eventually found the right potholed route to Plovdiv via Kostenets and Pazardzhik. It's about 100 miles and we weaved between Route 8 and the A1 motorway. We were looking for a cycle route to combine safety, practicality and speed. While Clive drove, I made shaky notes on road numbers, quality of surface, gradients and suitable stopping-points. A good deal of banter punctuated our earnestness. Taking an aged motorhome as support-vehicle/hotel/shelter/maintenance truck provoked much discussion as to how it would fare on dodgy roads. Cyclists can weave in and out of craters. Later we would seriously consider cycling on the wide hard shoulder of the motorway.

Our first stop was at a roadside bar/restaurant outside Kostenets. There were two shabby women and a shabby man having lunch outside. The terrace was an extension of the car park. We smiled and walked into the most basic of eateries. The peasant woman behind the bar, with scarf and housecoat, smiled and spoke Bulgarian. Clive responded with the usual Brit-reply. *Speak English?* A slight and hesitant shake of her head told us that, not only did she not speak English but she had no inkling of what Clive had said. The beer taps were before us. First things first. Clive raised two fingers, politely and we both gestured *large* by opening our hands and arms out. Smiles all round as full comprehension was registered.

The menu was a Cyrillic nightmare. Pointing to the hieroglyphics did us no good as our landlady's charade-skills were well below Clive's. After a short while we gave up, convincing ourselves that we weren't hungry anyway. Luckily giant bags of crisps were on display and so we simply pointed.

Outside the man scoffing his lunch had enough broken English to tell us that we were crazy. He confirmed that we were on the right road but pretty soon lost interest in the struggle for communication. We rejoined our car with crisp and beer belches forming the soundtrack of our departure.

The A1 and A4 motorways which take you to the border are smart dual carriageway style roads and the most obvious sign of EU investment. The hard shoulders are wide and peasant traffic and bicycles are allowed. We saw little of this type of transport but we noted the possibility of safe cycling on Bulgarian motorways. The gradients even out and the traffic is light for the most part. If a horse and cart can trundle up the side of a superhighway, why not three old Brits on bikes?

Coming into Plovdiv, Bulgaria's second city, Google maps swung into more effective action. By now early evening, the place was busy. Plovdiv has a population of over 300,000 and you can double that if outlying areas are included. The Bulgaria Star Hotel, a relic of communist architecture, gave us a warm and charmingly broken-English reception. We had parked our car illegally but were blissfully unaware of the fact. All we knew was that we were in central Plovdiv and the evening was ours to enjoy.

7
PLOVDIV TO EDIRNE:
THE RECCE CONTINUES

It might have been better not to have been on a flying visit to Plovdiv. The Roman and Greek theatres, the ancient stadium, the ethnographic museum, the parks and the rest would all have to wait. Clive and I, like two Russian agents in Salisbury, affected interest but had more important matters to attend to.

Central Plovdiv has an attractive, cobbled old town. EU money is helping to dismantle a creaking infrastructure. Giant diggers were excavating a huge underpass through the heart of the city. The Bulgaria Star opened on to a charming square just a stone's throw from the monumental earthworks. A balmy autumn evening ensured a happy throng of drinkers and diners. We gobbled down *Happy* food at one of the eponymous and ubiquitous chain of restaurants. *Happy* girls wear tight red tee-shirts and skimpy red mini-skirts. They smile unfailingly as they serve you. So too the boys - shorts rather than minis but the effect is, well, happy. The *Happy* place is a Wagamama with attitude and great table-service. And, yes, English was spoken, if broken. Praise the Lord.

The cafes were full. Urban Bulgars eat and drink out in considerable number - and at least as many women as men were quaffing vino and doing lunch or supper wherever we went. The night air filled with music from west and east but my lasting memory is of Elvis crooning *Are You Lonesome Tonight*. Few people seemed to be. There was a buzz about.

I had been rather idle on the foreign exchange front and had my cards but no cash. Clive had changed a certain amount but neither of us was quite prepared for how far his Bulgarian Levs would go. Think half price for almost everything. Outside Sofia hotels and taxis seemed even cheaper. We soon realized that Clive could pay for everything and I would settle up on return. Result.

We had had a long day. The itinerary for tomorrow involved a quick wander round Plovdiv, a visit to the Turkish consulate, driving on and walking across a traffic border into Turkey. Less than a week previously Jamal Khashoggi had been murdered in Istanbul.

We woke to the early morning buzz of central Plovdiv. We checked out of the Bulgaria Star and wandered to our car to find that we had parked it under a warning sign with a towing hieroglyph which resembled a hangman's noose. Inscrutable taxi drivers at the rank opposite grunted that we should escape sharpish.

Taxis and their drivers are everywhere. So too traffic wardens. In the absence of meters or that annoying system in UK cities of paying vast sums by credit card, the Bulgarian state employs thousands of quite sour-looking men and women to patrol city streets and sting motorists. A paltry wage, no doubt but employment nevertheless.

In a nearby street we found a neat parking slot and approached the parking police. After a humorous sign-language exchange we worked out that city-centre parking was 50p an hour. We surmised that our 3Lev would go straight into his pocket. To be fair and after a bit of a delay he handwrote a receipt. Of course, what it said was beyond our ken. Maybe, *Thanks suckers!*

We discovered the Turkish consulate. A bunker-like building down a side street. Several police heavies in combat-fatigues and threatening sub-machine guns were hanging around outside. There was banter. About Khashoggi perhaps? Clive approached the huge metal door and pressed the intercom. A crackling. Clive, with his best, mellow, apologetic London voice crooned, "Good morning...erm...do you speak English?"

A pause. The crackle restarted. Then a deep, resonant, growl, "Yes...a little."

Clive then gabbled about our being two gentlemen of the UK, on a planning mission for a cycle ride across Bulgaria and into Turkey. As we were unable to take our hire car across the border could we catch a bus to Istanbul or, at least the nearer town of Edirne? There was a silent patience as Clive prattled on. When he finally ran out of garbled explanation, there was a long pause before the electronic suction-whoosh of the giant door was remotely unlocked. We pulled back the heavy portal and we were in.

Faced with a couple of bored-looking but formidable guards and security-scanners, we both had the same thought: once inside, will we ever come out? We were ushered into a waiting area with a few young Turks queueing for attention.

A swarthy man appeared from a door behind us and approached. "You wait here. Someone see you soon." The same gruff voice of the intercom. He turned and disappeared through the same door.

Whilst we waited we noted a burly man in a very unfurnished office, sitting behind a desk. We soon confirmed that our imaginations were both working in similar overtime, visualising the special type of interview which was his speciality. Almost immediately the group in front of us stepped aside and a middle-aged woman appeared behind the grille.

Clive's manners were impeccable. "Hallo, do you speak English? Can you help us, please?"

"Yes of course. What can I do for you?" Pleasant, direct and smiling...or was it a grimace?

Clive then repeated our request. We wanted to see if we could catch a train or bus to Istanbul, that very day, from the border at Kapikule. Firstly we were encouraged. Trains and coaches went from Edirne, just over the border, to Istanbul. Our spirits rose.

"But the transport only goes overnight. Nothing in the day."

"Let me get this right," said Clive," Buses do go to Istanbul but only after ten at night. We can't get there in daylight today."

"I don't think so. We can do papers for car but it will take a few days. Sorry." All said with a genuine smile, actually.

Undaunted Clive persisted, "OK, can we park our car at the border somewhere and walk across into Turkey?"

"I don't know about car but yes, you can walk over border. Is unusual but not illegal. You have passport, you can go."

And with that we were done. We thanked our Turkish lady and, somewhat nervously navigated the exit-security, pleased to be the other side of the steel door and heading for coffee in the sun at a street café. We returned, briefly, to the Bulgaria Star to pay 3Lev (£1.50) for mini-bar water which we had overlooked. The receptionist was pleased and amazed at our honesty. British through and through.

We took Route 8 to Khaskovo out of Plovdiv. The road was flat and straight but started to climb as we reached a major fork in the road: left to Burgas and the Black Sea or right to the mountains and the choice of Macedonia or Greece. Route 8 was right but our road map of Europe suggested it later wended its way to the Turkish border. The new E80 motorway would also take us towards the Turkish border and the signs suggested a slip road in a few kilometres. We stuck to Route 8 in the hope that we would find a cosy, quiet border crossing manned by rustic, sleepy border police who would smile and joke incomprehensibly with us but wave us cheerily across no man's land.

In the event, after lunching in Svilengrad - again managing to choose a meal and beer via expert charades and friendly guffaws - we headed down a small road which we were certain would take us to the border. The traffic thinned and we passed pile upon pile of butternut squashes and pumpkins, stacked untidily outside forlorn farmhouses. Soon we were lone travellers heading for a sentry box, which we took to be the border.

An unshaven and unsmiling guard stepped out with arm raised. We gabbled our question, " Can we go across the border here?" Once again our clear English was met with a quizzical gaze. A young woman, in similar fatigues but looking a whole lot more formidable, stepped out from what looked to be a garden behind the sentry box. She managed to convey that this was where the road ended. Turn around, please or things could get tricky. Further, she explained that the border with Turkey was being *Trumped*; a fence of some 30km had nearly been completed. This to contain a surge of migrants from the Middle East and North Africa. The only official crossing point was the Kapikule motorway customs.

We did as we were told. We doubled back, found the road which linked to the motorway and headed past mile after mile of heavy freight traffic queueing to gain entry into Turkey. As we moved between Bulgaria (EU) and Turkey (non-EU) we observed, first hand, a border with friction. For several miles either side of the border, along the A4 motorway in Bulgaria, becoming the D100 on the other side, the carriageway was gridlocked with freight traffic backed up for access into and out of the EU at the Kapikule crossing. Each lorry takes fifteen minutes or so to clear, we were told. Good job the drivers had sleeping accommodation in their cabins and board games to while away the day, or more, that entry or exit would take.

Cars seemed to have fewer problems. We were a curiosity for Bulgarian and Turk border police. Little English is spoken at this edge of Europe and two near-septuagenarians trying to explain our plan to cycle from the UK to Istanbul next year, was stretching credibility in any language

We parked our car in a coach bay and walked to what looked like a toll booth. The Bulgarian border police clearly weren't used to ageing Brits strolling past the car queue with holdalls in hands and smiles at the ready. We found a guy in a khaki and green uniform, sporting the sort of captain's cap that Bing Crosby wore in *High Society*. He looked at us curiously as we began with a question.

"Can we walk over the border here?"

A studied silence, then a slow, deep drawl..."Yerrss."

"Can we leave our car over there in the coaching bay?"

This was a trickier question, requiring a couple of seconds thought and then a wry smile. "No...is illegal."

"We are only going a few miles into Turkey and coming back by tomorrow midday." We were grasping at straws here.

"Only one day?" he drawled suspiciously. "Well OK. Car is OK for one day."

Progress but we wanted confirmation, "So it will be OK to leave the car. It won't be towed away?"

"I don't think so. You leave. I check in morning. Is OK." He seemed satisfied and so were we...just. We picked up our bags and walked into the passport office, feeling rather like spies being quietly exchanged at the border. They had been alerted, clearly, that two odd pedestrians would need to be processed into Turkey. As we moved across some 300m of no man's land and into a similar passport-check-booth on the Turkish side, the scrutiny of our visas was rather more thorough. The Bulgars seemed pleased that we were heading out of their patch but the Turks seemed a little less keen to welcome us.

But enter Turkey we did. As promised a small bunch of taxis waited at the crossing, mostly to ship border workers to and fro. We found a smiling old chappie with whom there was no chance of meaningful communication. We wanted to go to Edirne, a small city just a few miles in from the border. My pronunciation of Edirne (*Ay-dear-neigh*) didn't find a flicker of recognition. Enter Google translate. The old taxi-man had done this before. We spoke English into an iPhone, he replied in Turkish. Mr Google then worked his magic.

We were on our way to Edirne and the Selimiye Hotel, just 200metres from the famous mosque of the same name.

***

Our lovely taxi driver dropped us right outside the hotel and a couple of hundred yards from the majestic Selimiye Mosque. We were slightly more rattled than he evidently was from the near-miss of another taxi having swung immediately across the front of his only half a mile before.

English was spoken by our charming host at the Selimiye Hotel. He had a Celtic look about him, light-skinned and fair-to-ginger hair. I'm not sure what I expected of a Turkish hotelier but he was certainly unlike his swarthier compatriots wandering around this lovely city.

We wandered to the mosque and the vibrant bazaar in its curtilage. Spices, sweets and clothing and colour. The displays were stunning in their sensual appeal and extraordinary neatness. On we went into the pedestrianised centre. Late afternoon and dusk was imminent. We waited for the call to prayer, expecting the happy throng of Turks to set a course for the mosque. The call came, loud and clear. Not a flicker of response. The cafes and shops remained buzzing as the prayer call echoed from the minarets and the city speakers.

We strolled past an inspiring, exciting fish market in the middle of town. We were searching for a much-needed beer after our border experiences. On and on we trotted. Plenty of coffee and hookahs about but after twenty minutes hard searching, no beer. We were contemplating the strangeness of a soft drink when a small sign which, unlike most, was immediately recognizable: *Bar*.

We sidled in to this little gem and, as the only customers, were greeted with some adulation. Another swarthy guy and his charming (and less swarthy) daughter smiled uncomprehendingly as we chirruped our one-word question, "Beer?" After a worrying pause I spied a large fridge stuffed with a variety of local and international brands of the amber nectar. A rapid and euphoric pointing at the fridge secured the required response. Big smiles all round and two giant bottles of a lovely chilled brew were on their way. We conducted a brilliant conversation with our hosts during which a good deal was said and almost nothing understood. Laughter abounded and the nibbles plate was regularly replenished, as were the beers. We will return.

That evening in Edirne confirmed that it would be a fine resting place on our pan European journey, whenever that may be. The following morning our trusty taxi man arrived on cue to whisk us back to the border. Clive's passport was barely scrutinized as we wandered out of Turkey. Mine, however was taken away for further analysis by a young, unshaven chappie, more guerrilla than border-force, I thought. He returned and grudgingly gave me back my identity.

We remained unsure as to whether our car would be waiting for us in the lorry/coach bay on the other side. An additional problem was our concern as to how we could cross the central reservation at the border to make our getaway back through Bulgaria on the right hand side of the motorway. As we walked through immigration we saw a gap in the border fence which would take us towards where we left the car on the other side. We looked around and all seemed well to nip through. As we marched towards freedom a gruff voice shouted. We assumed the translation would have been close to *Oi, where the bloody hell do you think you're going?*

About turn. A beckoning finger from a large, aggressive man. Cars were being routinely stopped and their contents rifled. It was clear that plenty of trafficking or other illegal stuff goes on at this gateway to Europe. When Mr Big opened our holdalls, the look of disappointment, indeed almost disgust, at our boring underwear, shaving gear and smelly socks, was comical. With a dismissive wave of his arm he indicated that he wasn't paid to bother with this trivia. He and the dogs went off to fry bigger fish.

And so through the fence and, glory be, our car was there. Not only that but a gateway allowed us to traverse the motorway and leave the border without further ado. Joy - and a fast road back to Sofia.

For the thirty six hours we were in Sofia we were relaxed tourists. The city has a great deal to offer with wonderful Roman ruins revealed in the city centre merged imaginatively with a new metro system. The market area is typically vibrant and horse chestnut trees abound. They are a health and safety wonder as most pavements have risen and ripped as the root systems of the great trees have wreaked havoc. Wonderful.

A Balkan country shaped by Ottoman, Russian, Greek, Slavic and Persian influences is bound to throw up cultural variety, inconsistency and extremes of fortune over the centuries. Lenin's statue was replaced in 2000 by Sveta Sofia's enormous monument, in the city centre. The pedestal alone is forty-eight feet tall.

There's much to see, of course, for the culture vultures. It's always intriguing how nations report their own history in their national history museums. We went to a charming national art gallery, the stunning Nevsky Cathedral, the ancient Church of St. George. Gardens abound and the city is green and lovely. A large crowd was gathered in a corner of the central park as we wandered through. What were they gawping at? A game of chess.

8
BACK TO BLIGHTY
CLIVE: "ARE WE SERIOUS?"

The journey back to Luton wasn't without incident. There are two terminals at Sofia Airport. Having been to one of these hubs a mere three days earlier it boded ill for our planned adventure that neither Clive nor I recognised the airport on our return. We tossed a coin; heads T1 Tails T2. Tails, so T2 it was...but we were wrong. Having parked in a taxi rank we now found ourselves blocked in by dozens of cabs waiting for the next incoming flight. They wouldn't budge. We needed to escape to T1 and get the hire car back - with all the palaver that invariably entails.

A dark, stubbled spokesman for the cabbies' union sidled up to us and suggested that Clive drive the tiny two door Clio up over the chunky kerb, along the grassy central island, slaloming the lamp posts seemingly placed for a bizarre advanced driving test and bump back down on to the exit road. I could only see the oil sump, petrol tank and exhaust being rent asunder. The taxi drivers, now excited at the prospect of a foreigner wrecking a hire car, gathered to spectate. I am not given to praising Clive but his skill in executing the concrete obstacle course outside T2 was a privilege to behold. Again, we made our flight from T1 with minutes to spare.

***

Back at home Chris was feeling underinformed and wanted to have a three-couple pow-wow. He set up our Eye To I WhatsApp group and tried to pin down his partners in crime to a summit meeting. The text conversation reads:

Chris: Clive, are you, Karen, Paul and Belinda able to come here for lunch on 19 Nov to plot our mission?

Clive: Sorry, we fly to Portugal, 19th - 26th.

Chris: 3rd December?

Clive: Fine for us.

Paul: No can do. We're planning a trip, Fri 30th - Sunday 9th.

Chris: *Fucking non-starter then. We're meeting the barge boys at the Antelope for Xmas beers. Can we debate the pros and cons over a pint or ten? BTW I now do a spin class early doors and, today, did a 30 miler in the Surrey hills. No pressure!*

Paul: *My bike has a puncture. Spinning? What's that?*

Chris: *Ha ha. I'm a spinning virgin. I'll explain when I see you.*

Well, we met at the Antelope in Surbiton, just before Christmas and had a very merry time with a large number of buddies. Naturally we couldn't fit in any time for a chat about cycling across Europe.

Clive needed final commitment; Chris needed questions answering; I was helpfully going with the flow. Christmas beers at the Antelope in Surbiton was proving to be a fruitless planning meeting until Clive asked, "Boys, I just need you to tell me before I fall asleep on the train back to Northampton. Are you with me or not? Are we serious about this?"

Chris had been placated by our reports of the ease with which Bulgarian roads could be ridden. Clive and I may have under-represented the problems a tad but what's a white lie between friends? We smiled beerily at each other and shook hands on it. No turning back.

Clive moved immediately into full combat mode. Maps, ferries, cycle books, airline schedules, bike bloggers, Eurovelo guides - you name it, Clive was going to read and research it. Or, rather, he had already done so. He had been putting in the hours of homework behind our backs. Swot.

He was worried, though, that we hadn't managed to get to Istanbul on our recce. After our fourth or fifth pint he turned to me and asked, airily, "Fancy a January jaunt to Turkey to suss out the road from Istanbul to the border?"

What could I say?

9
COUNTDOWN BEGINS IN ISTANBUL

1st January 2019. The New Year brought home the reality of it all. Clive sent us a tentative timeline of training and dates. We had to book ferries and flights and some campsites by late spring. Training should get under way sooner rather than later. The best time for weather and avoidance of heatstroke would be mid-September to mid-October. All this still had seemed a distant mirage during the frolics of Christmas but Clive was now focused. He had booked our recce flights to Istanbul for Sunday 13th.

Chris met the new year with characteristic resolve. He and Clive became research buddies, salivating over maps and routes and kit lists. For my part, I agreed to blog and photograph and publicise. On Sunday 13th Clive and I flew to Istanbul.

***

Chris's WhatsApp on 6th January had asked: *What's your agenda in Istanbul, chaps? Apart from an oily rub down with a Turkish driver's jockstrap.* Clive's reply was suitably crude and dismissive. Istanbul is a less mesmerising place in early January. It's about the only part of Turkey that sees snow. We landed at Ataturk airport in a flurry of the white stuff, picked up our hire car from a vast car park a mile or two from the terminal and headed into Sultanahmet, the vibrant touristy suburb of the great city which boasts the Blue Mosque and Hagia Sofia, the two great temples of Istanbul. Clive and I were more interested in beer and the excellent Turkish cuisine boasted by a large number of eateries trying to break even in the damp of a somewhat touristless January evening.

Our Hotel, the Acra, was an amazing construction, built over the ruins of Emperor Constantine's palace. These ancient rocks sit at your side in the basement which doubles as archaeological site and dining room. While we might have preferred a rooftop breakfast overlooking the Bosphorus, this was a pretty good second best. We dumped our bags and headed just a few chill metres to run the gamut of Akbiyik Cadessi, a street heaving with restaurants. Outside each eatery hovered insistent and smiling Turks wooing us into their gas-heated, awninged dining spaces. We succumbed to a charming jolly frozen stick of a man who promised us the earth. His teeth chattered and he warmed his hands over a brazier while pleading for our trade. His English was excellent; "My boss is inside; he married a girl from Huddersfield." With this intriguing information and his promise that we would always be his blood brothers, we entered. Later we would be promoted to his *fathers*. As luck would have it Man Utd were playing - and beating - Spurs and so my enjoyment of beers and shish kebabs was immeasurably enhanced. Not to mention the banter of the restaurant owner whose English accent was part Ottoman, part West Yorkshire.

Late night drinks in another bar and falling into company with a bunch of travelling misfits, Clive and I staggered back to the Acra in the small hours, somewhat unprepared for a full day's recce on the roads to the Bulgarian border. I had already spotted that Clive's driving could be suspect as he had scraped the front of our brand new hire car (another Clio) against the giant kerbstone outside the Acra. His grogginess as he fell out of bed boded ill for his abilities behind the wheel today. A good breakfast in Constantine's palace revived us somewhat and we headed out of Istanbul in fair fettle.

We had a couple of basic road maps. You know, the sort you buy from petrol stations where 100 miles is covered in half an inch. As navigator I could just discern the difference between the E80 (motorway) and the D100 (A road). We headed back past Ataturk airport, noting that there was a blue cycle path which ran from the outskirts of Istanbul for a few miles. It ran out of steam before the airport, as if the Turks had worked out that no one cycles away from an airport anyway. We saw no bikers and wondered if there was a fitness or environmental agenda which had lost its way. This amazing city is in the throes of huge building and infrastructure development providing a powerful contrast with an ancient world which was fighting for survival. We were to see, on the road to the border, an extraordinary amount of building of all sorts. What we had heard about the faltering Turkish economy seemed at odds with the pulse and modernity of what we saw. And in the months that were to elapse before we returned, the changes became ever more striking.

We checked into a hotel in central Lulebegaz, about 50 miles from the Bulgarian border. A small industrial town with little to commend it save for its ugly name. The concierge spoke a little English and happily taught us the few Turkish words and phrases which would help us access food and drink in the crowded hubbub of town. We had left our car in the hands of a toothless smiling vagrant who had flagged us down and into an Ottopark. The streets of Lulebegaz were chock-full of haphazardly parked vehicles, mostly with the dents and scrapes of multiple careless collisions. We hoped that the sanctuary of an Ottopark would prevent further scratching of the bodywork. We paid little attention to the maze of streets which led back to our hotel. By the time we set off for our evening meal, we had no idea where to find our car the following day.

Searching for beer proved, once again, to be a needle in a haystack adventure. I won't bore you with the details but after half an hour or so, we brushed aside the multicoloured plastic strips of a dingy side-street hole in the wall. A dark cavern filled with swarthy men playing cards, chess and drinking beer. We sat down and one of the swarthies stood and wandered over to us. *Bira* or *Efes* said confidently are words that make Turkish barmen spring into action. Indeed Efes is the most popular beer in Turkey and sold around the world. And yet devout Muslims eschew alcohol. The bar we had found was an old drinking emporium. Men only, low basso-profundo, growling conversations and only the occasional curious glance at the unusual sight of two ageing Brits supping ale in the middle of a Turkish town which rarely sees an outsider's face.

It only took about an hour to find our Ottopark the following day. Two minutes' walk from our hotel. We had seen enough of the road to Edirne so headed back to Istanbul. I made copious notes on roads, landmarks and, finally, a campsite spotted just off a service road outside Silivri, on the Sea of Marmara. Here we would hope to camp the night before our triumphant final cycle into Istanbul in a few months' time.

10
THE GRITTY MONTHS

We had each resolved to start our training in January. Fat chance. Wind and rain and inertia all contributed to our sloth. Ageing bodies are delicate machines that don't need the guts being thrashed out of them. My tyres were flat anyway. The WhatsApp and email exchanges in the early part of the year included rather pathetic boastings of work outs in gyms and mini bike rides. Clive cycled 10 miles on the 9th Jan and managed a one mile row in the gym. Istanbul here we come!

Chris and Clive efficiently raided appropriate bookshops and Amazon for variously confusing books - *The Danube Bike trail*, *The Danube Cycle Way* and *The Rhine Cycle Route* which starts at the source and therefore has to be read backwards if travelling west to east. Pictures of these, a cycle phone holder and a book by Neil Thubron called *Yucan* were WhatsApp-ed in January. Clive seemed impressed by the book which is a fist pumping guide to extreme adventure. Mr Thubron helpfully advised the seven Ps: *purpose, preparations, plan, pledge, perception, pain and persistence*. Clive commented that he found it useful. Can't say that I did. Clive responded by posting a pic of *The Man Who Cycled the World* by Mark Beaumont. I still wasn't impressed.

Tracking our communications in the first months of the year, you could be forgiven for thinking that it was all rather haphazard. As I reread, however, there was a steady and thoughtful build-up. We weren't going to peak too early, that was for sure, but each of us was mindful of increasing our physical activity. On 28th February the six of us lunched at *The Deer's Hut* in Liphook for a board meeting. This was the first time that we had all been in the same place, same time to chat nitty gritty and pipe up with reservations. As was to be the case going forward, this was a serious but fun meeting. We were fully committed and the girls were right behind us.

I started regular bike rides, say twice a week, in mid-May. A ten miler one day and something over thirty another day. Fair weather of course. And recording it on Strava meant that the boys could congratulate me with virtual high fives and fist pumps. In our own ways we each did what suited. Avoidance of injury gave each of us a good excuse not to overdo things.

There were business matters to attend to. Checking insurances for our delicate bodies, getting us all legal to drive the Mothership. Clive bore the brunt of this admin along with booking the Stena ferry from Harwich and the first couple of nights in Dutch and German campsites. Press releases were prepared and the blogsite set up. Clive exhorted us to contact local media, which, apart from Radio Northampton, showed no interest whatsoever. Three old gits traversing Europe on pedal bikes didn't rate highly against the big story - our divided nation leaving Europe.

Chris and Clive managed a meet-and-pedal in Northampton. Clive and I raced around Richmond Park with his son George who had flirted with the idea of joining us for a few hundred miles to Vienna. In the end he bought a narrowboat and occupied himself with canal matters instead. Chris visited me in Kent for a hectic and hilly thrash round the countryside. Just before he arrived at my place I discovered that both my tyres had exploded in the heat of the back of my car. RM Cycles in Tenterden came to my rescue with a lightning repair and I duly met Chris for a steamy 30 miler, followed by beer. We all managed to meet and ride in the Surrey Hills near Hindhead and Chris and I had our Mothership driving tests so we could head off for one practice overnighter before D-Day.

D-Day for Eye To I was to be Sunday 15th September 2019. The stars would be aligned, we were sure. Sunday morning would be the best time for us, friends and family to gather in central London. Mid-September to mid-October was about the best weather window for temperature across Europe. We might get unlucky but the timing was as good as we could get. The downside, we would later discover, was to be that campsites tend to shut up shop by the end of September.

I called these months the gritty ones for a reason. Once you know that you are going to do something you just want to crack on but the practicalities and the waiting tend to take the edge off anticipation. In addition, along with the delights of newly minted grandchildren arriving, elsewhere there was a good deal of death about. Four friends, yes four, died well before their time. I attended funerals in January, March and June of 2019. We all needed to crack on with living before our numbers would be up.

Clive launched the Eye to I Just Giving site for BeatSCAD in March 2019. We each determined that soft sell was our way and tended to advertise the charity only when asked. Slowly but surely our friends and family contributed. Within a couple of weeks Clive's modest target had been passed. What good people! We hoped that a blog diary on the trip would generate interest and money as we went along. We were thankful for the boost of cash and care.

11
ON THE BRINK

Only Covid 19 currently gets in the way of a barge trip and by June 2019, Coronovirus was more likely to be a video game than a world-changing pandemic. So it was that the Grand Union Canal was revisited by the Bargee boys in late June of that year. Training went out of the window as we spent the day at a beer festival near Foxton Locks, a lovely flight of locks which we saw through an alcoholic haze. Clive did some embarrassing Dad dancing in a pub garden marquee. Chris started to join in but soon regretted it and withdrew to the sanctuary of his pint glass. I filmed the whole sad charade. There's little to match a bunch of wrinklies making fools of themselves. This was not good for our training.

Neither was the Champions League saga, the World Cup, the Ashes, Wimbledon or the start of the football season with Spurs (Chris's unfortunate passion) installed in their new Stadium with Chris champing at the bit to use his season ticket. Distractions aplenty. Meanwhile Mother Theresa May was falling on her sword to make way for our trustworthy and well-groomed leader, Boris.

The lead up to our traversing Europe had the ironic backdrop of the gruelling Brexit saga. Whatever happy things were going on the gnawing, daily grind of our political chaos was wearing down the nation. The effects of this and the virus will be with us Brits beyond the time that the three old men on bikes are dust. We were thankful our European Union passports remained valid and that the Turks had seen fit to give us all visas.

Clive and Chris had liaised brilliantly over itinerary and by August Clive sent us the final plan of attack, which included the outline reproduced below which he also used as part of a press release, I think. Impressive anyway.

The salient bit for the cyclists gave us just a few butterflies!

Arrival in Istanbul, with 3 rest days, aims to be on Saturday 12th October. Estimation: 2580 miles (860 miles each)

DAY	DATE	JOURNEY	EST. MILES
1	15 Sept	London Eye to Harwich, Essex (C)	90
2	16 Sept	Hook of Holland to Millingen aan de Rign (C)	120
3	17 Sept	Millingen to Rodenkirchen (C)	120
4	18 Sept	Rodenkirchen to Mainz (C)	120
5	19 Sept	Mainz to Lohr a Main (C)	130
6	20 Sept	Lohr a Main to Bamberg	125
7	21 Sept	Bamberg to Regensburg (C)	125
8	22 Sept	Regensburg to Au (C)	120
9	23 Sept	Au to Krems (C)	125
10	24 Sept	Krems to Vienna (H)	120
11	25 Sept	*Rest day in Vienna*	Nil
12	26 Sept	Vienna to Bratislava (H)	45
13	27 Sept	Bratislava to Gyor (H)	50
14	28 Sept	Gyor to Visegrad (H)	80
15	29 Sept	Visegrad to Budapest(H)	40
16	30 Sept	*Rest Day in Budapest*	Nil
17	1 Oct	Budapest to Baja (C)*	120
18	2 Oct	Baja to Backa Palanka (C)	120
19	3 Oct	Backa Palanka to Zemun / Belgrade (C/H)	85-90
20	4 Oct	Belgrade to Dobra / Cevaza Beach (C)	120
21	5 Oct	Dobra to Gruia	110
22	6 Oct	Gruia to Montana	120
23	7 Oct	Montana to Sofia (via Vatsra) (H)	100
24	8 Oct	Sofia to Plovdiv (H)	100
25	9 Oct	*Rest Day in Plovdiv*	Nil
26	10 Oct	Plovdiv to Erdine Merkez (H)	115
27	11 Oct	Erdine Merkez to Silivri (C)	105
28	12 Oct	Silivri to Istanbul (H)	55
29	13 Oct	**Final cycle across to Asia and back	15

*C= camping, H= Hostel or Hotel ** Cycles not allowed to cross the Bosphorus on the bridges, so final crossing to Asia by ferry and a *short cycle 'around the block' in Asia before returning and finishing at the iconic Blue Mosque (Est 15 miles).*

***

My diary for the few weeks before departure seems to be filled with social and sporting fun. Chris went on holiday to Cornwall the week before we left. Clive went with Karen to the Transplant Games and I enjoyed a golfing holiday in Troon.

Chris's fondness for lists extended to providing a bullet-pointed survival pack. Top of the list, of course, was chamois cream. We had identified chafing as a potential game changer in our otherwise hopefully seamless progress to biking nirvana. This and a load of boring stuff such as lights for bike, torch, odometer, water bottle, back pack, glasses, energy bars...zzzz. I packed a weighty first aid kit, despite Clive's insistence that we had to travel light so as not to overcrowd the soon-to-be-beleaguered Mothership. One bag each, one pillow, a sleeping bag that could be scrunched into a tennis ball, one towel. And so it went on.

Our final meeting before lift-off was to be a recce of the route from London to Harwich and we had to spend a night in the Mothership to test our abilities to cohabit. One night should nail it. And what a night that turned out to be.

***

On 14th August we set off on our recce. I made scratchy notes as we bumped along in the Mothership. We picked up our route just outside the congestion charge zone going north east out of the capital. I made sense of these scribblings by texting the boys later. You can see just how professional an outfit we were. This prompted Chris to sign us all up to the iSharing app. He was certain that getting lost before we even left the UK was inevitable. With iSharing we could at least check on where an aged cyclist without a sense of direction might be located.

NOTES ON A TRIP TO HARWICH
Order of pedalling. Chris-Clive-Paul-Chris-Paul
Whether these notes make any sense, I'm not sure but here goes...
A1306 (NR13), Stop 1 to check all well after turning left at 0
A125 (Albion Pub)
Then rt. On to Ingreborne Way path after 200metres or so. (NR13)

Meet point shortly after Uxminster Bridge Station.

Leave 136 and head east B187. Under M25. Turn rt St. Mary's Lane. On to A128 and over 0. TR on to Billericay road (in Heronsgate)

After Little Busted, TL sp. Billericay, up Hatches Farm Rd, then L gain on to Tye Common Road. Farm shop lunch.

Straight thru Billericay. Left at Potash Rd. (rt 13 is off to the rt.) Van goes on and turns rt at 0 sp Chelmsford. Through Stock (13 should be going across at Stock) Stop 2

Go across A12. On A1007 TR at The Eagle. Route 13 should meet (coming from left) here at Watchhouse Rd. Cyclists TL at White Bear on Skinners' Lane; van straight on.

Follow signs to Colchester out of Gt Baddow (A12) then A414 Maldon. Through Danbury, TL for Little Baddow to meet Route 1 and stop 3. Route 1 on rt before Generals Arms where stop 3 will be.

Van and bike follow 1. At some point easier for van to go on main rd (A414?) Signage good for bike so few problems here. Into Maldon. Cycle route and van go through. At Rainbow House Chinese, cycles bear L. Van goes straight and takes B1022 out sp Heybridge, then Colchester.

At Great Totham Stores cycle path crosses. Van TL to join it. (T very shortly for Gt. Braxted) then rt again for Tiptree. Van doesn't have to follow NR1; 1022 Tiptree and Colchester.

Outside Colchester at 0 (bike route comes across in opp direction) continue on sp Colchester.

No further notes as the van and bike then have straightforward runs to Harwich, apparently! I don't have stop 4 details, so the stopping points need confirmation.

We cycled a little as we pottered along but the idea was more route recce than training. As usual peaking too early was high on our list of concerns.

We arrived at Dovercourt camp and caravan site on the outskirts of Harwich mid-evening. We had noted that a bar and restaurant was on site and had already fantasised about the size of steaks and range of beers that might be on offer. We walked into a Disneyland hell hole. A Bugs Bunny show for children was screeching unpleasantly on a makeshift stage. It was CBeebies writ far too large. The clientele was pushing squawking children towards the stage while they lined up pints of Fosters and snakebites, prepared to buy popcorn, chips and ice cream all evening to guarantee uninterrupted booze consumption. Real ale and pub grub was another country.

While Clive and I broke into smiles of benign resignation and prepared to down lager and chew burnt burgers, Chris asserted his authority. "Fuck this for a game of soldiers. I'm getting a cab into town." Chris had already asked the pleasantly vacant girl behind the bar whether proper beer was a possibility. And did they have an alternative menu to the heavily stained laminated burger and pizza list which he had picked up from the floor? Chris's optimism in the face of overwhelming evidence to the contrary was touching. When his hopes were dashed he was on a mission.

And so it was that we taxied to the Hanover Inn for a decent meal and decent beer. The locals were friendly and intrigued by our bike ride. Chris was like a pig in muck and started buying drinks for anyone who would chat to him. A chance comment by our landlord suggested that taxis after ten at night in the seething metropolis that is Harwich, might be a little thin on the ground. And so it proved. At least the pissing, driving rain of earlier had quelled somewhat but the three mile walk back to Dovercourt was a journey we could have done without. Luckily Clive and I aren't the sort to take the mickey out of friends when they've made small errors of judgement...

PART II
DURING

1
LONDON TO HARWICH
Sunday 15th September, 2019

The sun and excitement woke us early. Clive and Karen had stayed at Belinda's house in Cheam so four of us boarded the Mothership for the short drive to the South bank and the London Eye. A gaggle of friends and family appeared in Jubilee Gardens at the foot of the great wheel. Sebastian and Cressie, my lovely grandchildren, five and two respectively, were helmeted and raring to cycle and scoot the first few metres with us. The weather gods were smiling; if anything it was going to be a steamy hot day. We had planned parking, rendezvous and timings pretty well and the send-off was brilliant. We cycled a few hundred yards to the Mothership having waved our fans away. Little Sebastian managed to pedal along Upper Ground with us, past the Festival Hall. Then everyone melted away and we were left to rack up two bikes, before Clive and I waved Chris off on his bike towards Blackfriars and the whole thing began.

We had agreed the day's changeovers. Chris was lead-off rider, then Clive, Paul, Chris, Paul with Clive taking the early shift out of the Hook of Holland the following day. We were trialling the 5 or 6 leg model whereby each of us would have two stints in the saddle. After the first day we pretty much binned this as we all quite liked thrashing through our allotted daily mileage without having to think about another sweaty session later in the day.

We were heading north east to Harwich. On paper the mileage was easy - around 100miles. Getting out of London proved more tricky than Chris had imagined, however. He missed a turning or two (he won't admit to any more) and found himself farting around in the docklands and almost getting on the Woolwich Ferry. Clive recalls Chris *messing about round the Cutty Sark*. Clive had already headed off for the second leg by the time Chris pedalled into the Albion car park at the junction of the A13 and A125 in North London. The going was hot and slow.

The National Cycle routes are a well-mapped network of routes all over the UK. The signage, however, is at best patchy and at worst invisible. Luckily on our practice run we had navigated from pub to pub. The miniscule signs of Cycle Routes 13 and 20, which should have been our guiding stars were in little evidence for the obvious reason that the English are shit at providing enough cash to do things properly. Cycle signage may be an example. Added to this we don't appear to give much of a toss about cyclists. With all that has gone on in this second decade of the 21st century, things could be about to change.

It wasn't a straight line thing. Romford, Billericay and Chelmsford were skirted as we twisted and turned on country lanes. Chris and I were enjoying a cuppa at a farm shop a few miles from Maldon when Clive rode in alleging a puncture. His first ride on the odyssey and his green-slime injected super-tyres seemed to have sprung a leak. Using Chris's super pump, we instructed Clive to continue, saying that he must be imagining things. Chris and I settled back to our snacks before motoring on to meet Clive in Stock, from where I was to begin my own Eye to I effort. Clive soon appeared on the village green with green gel spurting from his front wheel and spraying our hapless party leader from head to toe. Cue laughter. We think Clive saw the funny side. In fact he even admitted to thinking that there was something funny about his front tyre a week before departure. Idiot.

Clive's version, written sometime later:

> I had a softening front tyre which was a puzzle - well, a puzzle to anyone who couldn't work out that it was a puncture! Colchester was fun for Chris again, finding that 'tolerant white van man' was keen to inform him that he was a 'flipping Charlie' or something similar! Paul, you seemed to have an interesting route when we (I think Chris and I) found ourselves crossing a 'Buses only bridge' twice for which an appropriate fine was initially proffered and, pleasingly, then rescinded when we told our story. Sadiq Khan, not so generous with the Low-Emission Zone penalty.

Again, more of the penalties which we were to incur across Europe, later.

My leg consisted of my following a road map and Google, the info from these being more comforting than the diminishing chances of cycleway signs showing themselves. Through Maldon (delightful) before Chris took over to Colchester. Getting in and out of this garrison town proved tricky, given that we had scheduled another takeover in the middle of it.

Clive and I drove round in circles looking for Chris, even though we were texting and chatting to effect a rendezvous. During the Mothership's contorted city centre twistings, Clive managed to pick up two penalty charges for entering a bus lane and driving up a one-way street. His story differs fractionally but you get the gist. Blissfully ignorant of this at the time, he drove on erratically until we located a sweaty Chris. I took again to my bike to pedal the last leg to Harwich. By the time the next few thousand miles had been travelled we would discover just how many fines we had incurred in various countries across Europe.

From Colchester the cycle signs were exemplary. Well done to whichever council or local cycling group did the necessary. By now we were a tad tight for time as the contortions of our journey from London had taken nine hours or so. We got to Parkeston Quay in darkness but in good time to enjoy the loud banter of three coachloads of Dutch stock car fanatics who, having had a grand weekend of racing, were hell-bent on partying on through the night ferry to the Hook of Holland. We felt our age as we ordered a modest bottle of beer each and headed for bed in the maze of dungeon-like cabins below decks. Stena had refurbished the accommodation and, apart from the usual difficulty that any sixty-seven year old might have clambering into a narrow top bunk, we all slept like logs. Chris was under me as it were and Clive, being tour leader took the solo room. Of course.

He paid for this luxury by having to pedal off the ferry at first light (notice the language of the intrepid explorer) in the insistent drizzle which is a Dutch speciality. It took him a while to locate the cycle path into Rotterdam, but locate it he did. Predictably he found that cycle shops are as common as colds in the flatland of Holland and he soon found a cheerful man with a spanner to repair his tyre and de-slime his wheels. Our three repair kits remained unopened and were to remain so for the whole trip.

2
MILLINGEN AAN DE RIGN

Now the Dutch know a thing or two about cycling. Their cycle paths are actually cycle paths and not white-line death traps at the edge of teeming A roads. The Eurovelo 15 cuts east across from the coast to the German border at Millingen. Flat, safe and fast. The Mothership invariably found herself having to drive considerable distances snaking around the protected cycle routes. Chris and I decided, while Clive was farting about getting his puncture repaired and his bike de-slimed, to grab coffee and culture at the extraordinary Windmills of Kinderdijk. Nineteen of them with pumping stations, dykes and reservoirs which control the flooding of the polder. Well, there's only so much fun to be gained in the steady rain and wind of South Holland, so the coffee lasted longer than the sightseeing.

I checked the Man United score from the previous night. Rashford's penalty beat Leicester. In the brave new world of Coronavirus lockdown, this young man would go on to win the hearts of the nation by persuading Boris to fund school meals for the needy through the summer of 2020. As our story goes to print, young Marcus has just been awarded an MBE and rightly so!

The other newsworthy items of our first cycling day included the farting contest that was held in India, apparently to normalise the practice of evacuating unpleasant smells. Also the rather more prosaic news that the Liberal Democrats had adopted a cancel Brexit policy. They did well with that didn't they? Writing, with the benefit of both hindsight and the irony of current events will, maybe, give a different spin on the story of our journey.

We had agreed that our daily rotations would ensure that we took turns to take the dawn, midday and evening shifts. Dawn = circa 6.30, midday = midday and evening = before 7pm. We had agreed that cycling in the dark would scare us, although the occasional mistiming or poor map reading would give rise to some twilight pedalling. We were also certain that our rides would have to overlap. Rider 2 would have to set off before Rider 1 had arrived at a checkpoint.

And so it was that I hopped on my Halford's basic at Kinderdijk and Chris waited for Clive to pitch up on his new wheel. We were travelling due east to pick up the Rhine on the German border. The rain gave way to hazy sunshine and we crossed the River Masa or Maas by ferry, the first of many landing-craft type vessels criss-crossing the rivers and canals of Europe which we were to encounter. When Chris took over from me he cycled through Arnhem where flags were flying from seemingly every building to commemorate the Battle of Arnhem 75 years earlier and the subsequent liberation of The Netherlands. Chris told us that he took a photo of what he thought was the bridge too far but which turned out to be the allotment too near. Our judgement of distances, handover timings and difficulties of terrain was mostly accurate but occasionally wayward. So it proved for Chris on his leg. He was still twenty miles from Millingen with darkness descending. We hastily agreed a meeting at a petrol station which boasted a MacDonald's. Chris kept bleating about road works hindering his progress but he did produce of picture of himself wading through sand and over ditches to reach his Big Mac. The automated menu in Dutch was yet another challenge. Undaunted, Clive managed three courses.

It was dark when we made it to our campsite, Camperplaats T Crumptse Hoekje, which nestled on the banks of the great river. The first day was done. We had beer on board - a present from Clive's American relatives and therefore, unreliable. However their Bourbon was to prove a nightcap hit...until it ran out. We had to negotiate our first night in the Mothership and our collective memory on how to set up the cosy double that Chris and I were sharing was sorely lacking. And so it was that we created a slatted base with large gaps, through which Chris's rather sensitive spine was to sink in the small hours. It was a tad chilly and Chris's inner boy scout had misread the need for a sleeping bag that was warmer than a duvet cover. As for Clive, well his first clamber using the swinging rope ladder wouldn't have won any prizes in a Tarzan contest.

We had known each other for over fifty years and being sporty, beery boys, our sensitivities had been dulled by decades of piss-taking. The linguistic pattern of our narrow-boating adventures had confirmed sarcasm and farting as the preferred utterances. The talent for not taking offence is to be treasured and Clive, Chris and I displayed Olympian levels of restraint as we batted unpleasantnesses across the Mothership as the first night drew on. Chris made it to 3am before the chemical toilet beckoned. Once his bladder had woken him there was no hope for Clive or me. Chris chuntered on pathetically about sliding down a hole in the slats and Clive begged us to hold his ladder steady while he regained the crow's nest. This pattern was to repeat itself for the month, even when we took to hostels and hotels.

3
MICROBURGERS

Clive's short term memory was already becoming the subject of humour. Now, granted he had a lot to remember but, if he had a system for not looking like a dick because he had again mislaid his glasses, it wasn't evident. He had two sets of Mothership keys. One set was always lost. His Specsavers glasses case was identical to mine; further cause for confusion and trauma. Pens, water bottles, padlocks, van keys, energy bars, cycling shorts, maps, wallet, phone, tickets, bottle opener, clothes...all these were on a merry-go-round of disappearance, with Clive calmly frustrated and perplexed by his inability to find what he needed in the moment. He has considerable form.

The Mothership required us to follow a routine of start-up and shut down so as to ensure safety and continued battery health. Microburgers was our checklist acronym : Microwave on floor, Battery console switched from Leisure to Engine (or vice versa), Urinal closed down, Refrigeration, Gas on/off, Electricity and Roof (close it!). Clive had tested us before departure and we were not found wanting. The van had a few quirks such as the electricity panel indicating red when all was well. It was as if the Mothership wanted to keep us on our toes. Good for her.

Of course we were having to rely on the old van not only as our support vehicle but as hotel too and the old girl needed cosseting if she were also to make it back to the UK afterwards. About 7000 miles in five weeks or so was a stretch for the old lady. Chris had already shown himself to be pretty heavy on the accelerator pedal in the Surrey hills and Clive pleaded for TLC and a maximum speed of 6omph while Chris's conversion to kilometres added a few revs to his calculation.

Our seating pattern would become the standard. Two in the front seat and one reclining in the lounge section unbelted. Clive's wife, Karen, had nagged him about ensuring that the rear seats were configured properly so as to ensure regular seat-belting. Well that went out of the window in favour of comfort.

The old lady rumbled along with a thunderous roar and a crockery-ringing jangle of moveable inner parts, each competing for the highest decibel score. The two small inner tables, balanced on metal spindles, were hinged so they could swing this way and that. And they did. Being in the rear of the vehicle as it trundled along involved rescuing books, papers and coffee cups from sliding off these unstable surfaces. There were plenty of moments of rear cabin drama but the closest to real disaster was when there had been a MICROBURGERS malfunction and some idiot had left the weighty microwave on the draining board. Yours truly rescued the machine as it started to topple off the counter, having been edged off by the erratic nature of Chris's driving and the reverberating throb of the Mothership.

Clive had allocated each of us about one square foot of storage. For Chris and me this amounted to two small holes, the size of glove compartments, above head height at either side of the cabin. We shared a wardrobe space which, being two feet wide, took our wet weather gear and a pair of jeans each and not much more. Clive filled his sleep compartment with his own junk. Naturally each morning became a rooftop scrabble to find all manner of things which he had mislaid from the night before. We each had fluorescent gear to make us visible and professional looking. The truth was otherwise, of course. Karen had funded BeatSCAD aerodynamic tight-tops and tee shirts for casual advertising whenever we were out and about. Clive had also bought three European Union flag shirts which we wore quite proudly. On Brexit, the three of us were on the same page: *Remain*. Water under the bridge now, or rather the economy. As for washing clothes, we were to encounter problems such as the stench of rancid cycle gear. Padded shorts may absorb some of the undercarriage pounding that bumpy and cobbled cycleways engender but they also absorb and retain the body odour of the nether regions. Unpleasant to say the least.

Our provisions were stored at the back of the van. We travelled light with cereals, pasta, milk and beer being the essentials. They have shops on the continent so we figured that buying everything else as we went along would not prove a problem. We each knew enough about such ventures that nutrition would be important. *Nutrition, nutrition, nutrition* a friend, Steve Shaw, had chanted at me as we talked in Troon on a golf jolly a month or two before departure. This good advice translated into cereal, tea and orange juice before the morning ride (the non-riders might stretch to egg and beans on toast), a baguette lunch and a campsite cafe blow-out in the evening. With energy bars, chocolate and regular hydration (yes water really works) this simple diet would see us through. We hoped.

4
INTO GERMANY AND INDUSTRIAL RHINELAND

Basil Fawlty's now outlawed piece of comedy racism was on our lips as we crossed into Germany at Millingen. We were unaware at what point The Netherlands finished and Germany began. Not difficult to reflect on just how wonderful a world without frontiers might be. As we were to discover to our surprise there would be plenty of borders within Europe. Also, almost as many currencies as countries. The Eurozone differs from the EU and there are several countries which would call themselves European, not in the EU, Serbia for one - we had to buy Serbian Dinars. A man in a currency booth in Tunbridge Wells had provided Hungarian Forints, Romanian Leus, Bulgarian Levs, Turkish Lira and Croatian Kuna. Plenty of Euros too. Remote locations required cash; otherwise plastic was fantastic.

Having enjoyed Clive's accounting methods on our recces, i.e. he paid for everything and gave me a bill at the end of the trips, we decided on a little black book approach. Whatever we spent went into the book. From petrol to beers to hotel bills - in it went. Chris was to produce a spreadsheet a couple of weeks after our return which detailed the damage and the payments which had to be made to equalise contributions. And so it was that we didn't really chat about money at all.

This account will rely on evidence pieced together rather haphazardly. None of us wrote a diary. Somehow the grind of a daily scribbling with the sort of detail needed to prepare for a proper retelling of the tale seemed rather a dull prospect and would certainly get in the way of evening beer, bedtime reading and opening our eyes to all that was around us. Days were packed and eventful. Nights were for relaxing. We did take photographs and we put short videos and blogs on Facebook and our website. In recreating the trip we have since sat around staring at our itinerary and maps with beers in hand saying things like, "Clive was it you who drove like a maniac on to the Millingen ferry? Or was it Chris? Or did we even take a bloody ferry?" An aged man is but a paltry thing wrote W.B. Yeats. The power of our paltry collective memories just about managed to recall most of it.

We were heading for Rodenkirchen, outside Cologne. The sun was glinting on the muddy Rhine as I took off early. A few thousand miles away Donald Trump's impeachment hearing was starting. Wishful thinking by the Democrats, I guess. We greybeards hoped that our modest challenge would have a better result.

It looked as if I might get the best of the cycling as my stint seemed to be riverside for much of the way until we hit the industrial corridor which runs from Duisberg, via Dusseldorf to Cologne. The Rhine is a mighty beast of a river, in part majestic when it courses through the lush green landscape of rural northern Germany; largely brutal and metallic as it cuts through the industrial heartland of central Europe. The Eurovelo cycle path isn't a continuous delight. We were to find that EU money was being variously used throughout EU countries to fund infrastructure projects both great and small. The progress on these depended, as a Hungarian observer was later to suggest, on the amount of political corruption. Our Rhine Guide, being read backwards of course, did not predict the regular cycle path upheavals. The three major river routes, plus a couple of canals that we would encounter, each required significant deviations from the waterside. Mostly these would be a pleasant detour through villages or fields before re-joining a towpath. Occasionally we had to set off up steep gradients and cycle a few circuitous miles before getting back on track; sometimes a deviation proved a blessing as we cut across long river bends.

On Day 3, I recall a blessed first leg. Forty miles or so of sunshine and good tarmac. Of the three of us I was easily the worst map reader. My sense of direction, having deserted me when I was about forty, was probably the thing which most concerned me. Otherwise I tended to be rather oblivious to the day's challenges. However, because I am likely to study a map for ages before pointing my bike in exactly the wrong direction, I insisted that I took all available charts with me, stowed in my back pack, rather like a child needs a favourite teddy to accompany him everywhere. In addition, I was ever eager to keep my phone fully charged so that contact with the Mothership could save me in the event of any catastrophic incident. Chris and Clive both seemed happy to jot a few notes down to slide into their see-through plastic pouches, which perched pretty sloppily on their handlebars. These scribblings and Google Maps seemed to satisfy. For me, I needed the full library of European cartography. Belt and braces. The downside of this strategy was (a) too much information and therefore (b) time-consuming stops to double check at least three different authorities on the correct route. Given that socking great rivers were often in sight, my worries seem, in hindsight, rather foolish.

Chris took over for a rather more gritty ride into - and out of Duisberg. He recalled it as follows:

> Duisburg, city with the largest chemical works in Europe. And I saw most of the huge number of plants. Getting in to the city was no problem. Despite, seemingly sensible people directing me, I lost the route completely on the way out. Clearly the road I found was used only by factory workers. Cue, Google Maps. Sensibly takes me shortest route to get back on track. Only problem it was a major route where cyclists are banned. EVERY vehicle hooted me while flying past within a cat's whisker. Little did I know, this was to be good practice for the Balkans! Arrived in a town which can only be described as Pleasantville. Lost in it as no signage at all and no one who spoke English until I flagged down a young lad on a bike who spoke beautiful English and even knew where the Rhine was, unlike all the old twats who I had had the misfortune to stop before! Relief on arriving in Dusseldorf to meet Paul and M'ship.

> Final note on Duisburg, my father was a gunner in Bomber Command - DFC incidentally - and the Ruhr was, of course, one of his hunting grounds during the latter part of the war. More than once, whilst in Duisburg, I silently wished that this place had never been rebuilt. Nasty, I know but....

> Day three - final note. Germanically run campsite. Umpteen generations of the same family - pictures of them all on reception wall. Kellermans of Dirty Dancing fame sprang to mind!

The 'Kellermans' welcomed us into their bar and made sure that we were topped up with ale until a table became available. We chatted to locals who were intrigued by our challenge (small picture) and perplexed by Brexit (big picture). The few Dutch to whom we had spoken couldn't make out the UK psyche; mind you, neither could we. The Germans were much more prepared to offer their own explanations for us. Somehow they recognised the argument that the great European project might not be in everyone's interests. Certainly one genial

Bavarian offered the thought that propping up the Greek economy wasn't very popular in Deutschland. They were well-informed and had much enjoyed seeing the bear-pit cauldron of Commons debate and, particularly, the growling of 'Order, Orrrderrr!' by our dishevelled Speaker, John Bercow. This Westminster pantomime was seen as an endearing quirk of a dotty nation. As we headed east towards the Balkans, Brexit appeared to be of little interest. I am not sure that the EU was high on the agenda of the average Romanian, either.

5
TO MAINZ AND LOHR: SWAPPING RIVERS

A video on our Facebook site of Clive answering silly questions from me, reminds me of the start of Day 4. His praise of the warm welcome we had been given already was to set the pattern for the whole trip. At Rodenkirchen the belching smoke of the factories outside Dusseldorf and Cologne had given way to a rural calm. A barge was sliding by like a pencil in a bath. A sparkling day was dawning as Clive set off to skirt Bonn. We were heading for Mainz and would turn off the great Rhine. Chris was in the saddle second and I would be pedalling the last leg. If the paths and roads were straightforward and in good order we could average 15 or 16 miles an hour. If the track was fast, straight and downhill that speed could be doubled for a few seconds before ageing reserve/fear set in and the brakes applied. Inclines, map reading, snack breaks and getting lost managed to bring down our mileage strike rate to around 10 miles an hour. It varied but it was rare for one of our saddles not to be warmed for about twelve hours each day. And this didn't include the necessary overlapping that was needed to get to our target destination each evening in the light. We all wanted to smell the roses, however. Clive invariably arrived with enjoyment written across his face. Chris has a sharp antenna for sights of interest, the detail of his surroundings. We all enjoyed engaging with those whom we met along the way.

Each day we knew by lunchtime if our planned destination for the evening was achievable. Clive had a list of campsites which might serve our needs and we would phone ahead to see if the place was open and had space. There was a fair amount lost in translation but we Brits should be more than ashamed at our expectation of others to speak our lingo. That many do - and apologise for their own 'poor English' - does them great credit. Almost all our conversations in shops, on the street, in cafes and on campsites began with the polite and apologetic, "Excuse me, I'm sorry to trouble you but do you speak English?"

Clive and Chris had checked in with Camping Maaraue in Mainz. I arrived via a series of interconnecting wooden bridges which led from the riverside, through a housing estate and across a couple of tributaries to the shabby but welcoming site, in mid-river. Our genial host was a German hippie with a long, grey pony tail and a twinkle in his eye. His beer was good: cold and cheap. The showers in almost all these strange locations were clean, refreshing, restorative. I recall, unfortunately, some pasta mush which Clive cooked up for filling our bellies. At least we would be carbo-loaded.

It was a pity that we had no time to explore Mainz. I had caught a glimpse of the octagonal tower which tops the Romanesque Mainz Cathedral. The town was also the birthplace of printing and Gutenberg is honoured with his very own museum. Presciently, as I type, Liverpool have just nailed the 2020 Premiership. Jurgen Klopp is a celebrated alumnus of *Mainz 05*, the club he played for and managed. His famous teeth were a much loved and regular sight on the streets of this Renaissance town. The old men on bikes, not being fans of the scousers and having been taught at school that William Caxton was the father of printing, felt that we could only do limited sightseeing at the numerous stopping points on our long journey. We gave Mainz a miss.

Day 5 was going to be a long one. Clive would manage two stints as he was feeling embarrassed that his odometer bore witness to fewer miles than either Chris or I had cycled so far. Perhaps he was confused by the conversion from miles to kilometres. I must say kms do click away nicely and buoy up a British rider who is used to the slow slog of mileage. Clive's early morning stint took him south of Frankfurt, to Wertheim and he would later manage a second ride into Lohr. When we turned onto the River Main we were immediately into a smaller and more captivating landscape.

The Main is a beautiful river with quaint riverside villages and vineyards rising to the hills. Hillside schlosses dot the horizon to right and left. The small ferries, like landing craft, which took us from one side of the river to the other, were a breezy delight. A Euro for a five minute river cruise. One day was beginning to merge into another but the Main gave us a different and more intimate experience. A crow would have made it to Wertheim and on to Lohr in no time but we were pleased to enjoy the speedy yet meandering towpaths in the gentle sunshine. Let your finger follow the Main on a map and almost every village or town that you encounter will have a charm all its own. Wine is the business of this rural watery corridor but pleasure boats and happy tourists patrol the river.

Each of us took time out to sit at riverside cafes with coffee or ice cream and soak it all up.

We had taken to whooping and fist pumping when a rider rode in or away. I noted that this all seemed rather unbecoming of aged men but, I guess, we all need an adrenaline tactic to big us up. Clive's arrival in Lohr was late and he struggled to locate Campinplatz Mainufer at the end of a rather shabby riverside industrial park. We feared that we might be out of luck for beer and food and have to resort to Clive's inexpert heating of dried pasta. Until, that is, we found a dodgy looking cafe/bar that seemed to be heaving with punters. Chris, our sniffer-outer of beer and carbs sent me this note recently.

Gorgeous day, and a long, beautiful ride, including wonderful views of the epic Schloss Johannisberg in the glorious sunshine. Great evening, having found a buzzing pizza restaurant that neither of you thought was a goer as it was so busy, until I persuaded you that if we just went in, had a beer and then take it from there we might get a table later. A menu of 80 pizzas. Great beer and a table within 5 minutes. Waited upon by the original German wench with an encyclopaedic knowledge of the menu and a memory to match.

My brief notes ran: Local hub restaurant, heaving. Ragged woman; brilliant English; memory like an elephant. Fun.

The video post on Facebook captures the buzz of the pizzeria. We felt blessed to have stumbled across such an atmosphere of relaxed fun. Evenings like this were to fuel our spirits as well as our bodies - and there were many more such weird and uplifting evenings ahead.

6
STRANGE NIGHT IN ELTMANN
Friday 20th September

We were heading to Bamberg via Wurzburg. Chris cycled off with simple instructions on how to navigate the mildly labyrinthine matrix of paths and rickety wooden bridges into town and then the towpath to Wurzbug. He remembers it like this.

Chilly morning. Paul explained how easy it was to find the river over the old bridges. So I got lost in the awakening town, but helped by a lovely mum taking her nipper to school. Another enjoyable day on the charming Main, criss-crossing it to take photos of the trains for my Thomas the Tank Engine potty grandson, Rex.

Evening in a one horse town with no bar, the name of which I cannot remember as I won't be going there again. Bizarre hotel, very piney and totally deserted apart from us. The hub of the town was a bang average Greek restaurant - but there was beer!

This was a pretty tough day as we had underestimated how many extra miles the twists and turns of the river (plus detours) might add. Another lovely day but headwinds were becoming a feature. With the wind behind I would be sailing along, upright like one of the Famous Five on a mission of adventure; a bend in the river and I metamorphosed into a panting, crouched, drop-headed rider battling an invisible element. Clive foresaw that we might not quite get to Bamberg and booked us in to a B&B, the Pension Maintal, in Eltmann, a few miles short of where we had hoped. The run into Bamberg, along the last stretch of the Main before we transferred to the Danube Canal would be no problem the following day. Famous last words.

We felt that we deserved some pampering by the time Clive cycled into Eltmann, a small town with few distinguishing features. A square, a church and nowhere open, apparently, at 7pm. The Pension was a hotel like the one run by Jack Nicholson in The Shining. Well, it had more timber than a ski lodge and its very incongruity in this granite town lent a slightly disturbing atmosphere to our sojourn. There was no one in reception but a number to call written on a scrap of paper by a bell on the desk. We phoned; a woman answered. A man would be along in five minutes. The man turned out to be a concierge/odd job man/barman rolled into one. There was beer in a locked glass-fronted fridge at which we had been gazing, longingly, in the foyer. Language once again proved to be no barrier. Beer was released!

We were shown to a suite! Well, a single bedroom, a double, a corridor and a bathroom. Chris's fastidious/privacy/anal gene came to the fore as he commandeered the single room whilst paying lip service to free choice. There was no drawing of lots. He said that he deserved a little luxury having had to endure the 'bum crack of a bed' in the Mothership.

We wandered into the deserted square fearing that we might have to rescue some sustenance from the Mothership. At the far corner, in the shadow of the church, we saw a light. A Greek restaurant. Of course! Souvlaki, moussaka, ouzo and beer followed.

I was off early next day and the video shows a chill morning of bright sunshine as I headed towards Bamberg with Chris's complaints of an uncomfortable bed making the early morning stint all the more pleasurable.

My pleasure was soon to turn to pain. My run into Bamberg was supposed to take a couple of hours. That was before a combination of road works detours and poor signage led me a longer and not very merry dance. The road works meant that one side of a rectangle turned into three as I had to turn at right angles to the River (Main) and steer uphill into charming villages and then work my way back down to the river. After a couple of these detours I worked out that I might as well just take the main road, despite the heavy traffic. This was not before I had followed a Eurovelo sign through a farmer's field and along a rutted track for three or four miles before coming to a dead end. I could see the river but the vegetation between me and it was impenetrable. Google maps hadn't been much help either. I texted the boys to give them updates but I was in remote territory and several messages didn't get through. Long story short, I was late. But we were in Bavaria and the locals were friendly.

Bamberg, when I got there, was a delightful place to see in the sun. The Romanesque cathedral and the medieval Rathaus (Town Hall) dominate the old town, which was thronging with tourists, students and day trippers. A friendly copper pointed me (vaguely) in the direction of the Donau (Danube) Canal, before admitting that he was part of a reinforcement group sent from a few miles away to help police an arts and music festival. He had last been to Bamberg as a child. At least he knew where the canal was.

And so we said farewell to the River Main and I handed over to Clive a couple of hours later than scheduled. Clive now had to get a head of steam on the Doanaukanal which connects the River Main with the great Danube. Headwinds meant that he struggled to make up the time, although the cycle path was pretty straightforward, the only hazards being eccentric cycleway signs and a combination of bridges which had to be traversed to access good tarmac first on one side of the canal, then the other. As Clive skirted round Nurembourg, Chris went shopping.

Whilst waiting for a shattered Clive, I ambled into a lovely town south of Nurembourg to find a supermarket. Gorgeous, hot day. Confused at the supermarket where food and alcohol were in separate buildings and you paid in one place and heaven help you if you put your food trolley in the alcohol trolley park - which I did. Cue, nice German man to the rescue.

Chris did accept that this is an extremely boring story. I include it just to show how difficult it has been to sort the wheat gems of memory from the dull chaff. After the trivia of supermarket trolleys Chris was to have the first serious problem of the trip. There had been plenty of cyclists around so far, loosely categorised as either amateurs or professionals. We looked like pros but looks can be deceptive. However, there are amateurs out there who have a kamikaze death wish. Chris found one.

I was nearly written off just west of Kelheim minding my own business, enjoying a gentle ride along the Danube after the rigours of the gravel paths and headwinds on the canal. On a narrow bridge and a maniac cyclist, head down, full tilt at me, not looking at all. I froze, trying to find somewhere to hide out of the way of this onrushing racer. I screamed when he was about 5 metres from me; he looked up, swerved, gored me in the thigh with his handlebars and skidded out of control along the bridge. In shock, I went back to this groaning, bleeding - no helmet - wreck of a 40 odd year old man, who was yelping like a whippet, blood pouring out of his ear. His "friends" who arrived slowly on the scene stood dumbly over him. Not English speakers. I think they were thinking "can't believe it, he's done it again" because they were so unconcerned. I managed to find an English speaker, told them to call an ambulance and then said "cheerio, I'm off. Hope he's ok". I could happily have taken retribution on the poor, whimpering idiot but didn't fancy an international incident, with the emergency services on the way. A lot of very fast peddling, on adrenaline, to the farmyard campsite. Very dark by then. I still have the handlebar mark!

Chris explained that his two-wheeled bridge attacker very much needed hospital treatment but his cycling mates seemed more put out than concerned. After some ten minutes or so Chris worked out that if police and ambulance arrived then questions would be asked, statements would need to be made and a right palaver might ensue. So he did what all right minded cowards would do. He scarpered.

Chris was somewhat befuddled as he (eventually) found our extraordinarily rustic little campsite, in Kelheim outside Regensburg. The entrance was a stable yard with a vast barn filled with hay bales and homemade swings, slides and ladders - a child's delight and a health and safety nightmare. Kids were leaping around playing some version of 'pirates' (remember that?) and completely unsupervised. Their hippie-like parents were in the field beyond sipping ale and smoking wacky baccy. Beer was in the campsite fridge and tonight we were to 'enjoy' another of Clive's culinary specials. There is pictorial evidence of the barn, tractors and the three old men smiling in the Mothership. Chris kept fussing about his bruising and came out with some claptrap about keeping his near-death experience a secret from Sarah for the time being. By the time he was on to a second beer he had rethought his sympathy strategy and had contorted himself to take a picture of his burgeoning bruise to send to his beloved.

One week down.

7
FAREWELL TO GERMANY

We were looking forward to meeting up with the girls in Vienna and taking stock, enjoying the sights and slowing down for a few days. While we were trundling and pedalling along we were in a bubble. We were aware of news from around the world but each day was a heads-down affair of basic concerns: nutrition, hydration and pedalling from dawn till dusk. It might appear that evening alcohol played a huge part. Not so really. A couple of beers or a glass of wine (Clive's Bourbon soon bit the dust) was enough to make our knackered bodies succumb to gentle slumber. Well, gentle enough until the chemical toilet called. A week in and the slatted bed remained a construction mystery. How we all wished that we had played more with our Meccano sets when we were lads. Nevertheless, we had established a comfortable platform for Chris's vulnerable spine. He was a happier chappie, despite continuing to complain about the low tog rating of his sleeping bag.

Cycling fans who might be reading this may develop a somewhat sneering view of our English amateurism. We rather enjoyed the stiff upper-lippedness as we set out on our solo journeys. There was invariably a Captain Oates style exchange ('I am going now. I may be gone for some time') as a rider set off. Equally there was a hyped and excited congratulation on return as if something extraordinary had been achieved. Tea was made, biscuits produced, the bike racked - red carpet treatment for the weary soldier.

Notwithstanding these histrionics we were ever mindful of keeping our bodies in fair order. While we didn't go overboard with early-morning stretches, we each had our warm-up routines, our pills, potions and creams-for-nether-regions. We each chose snacks and drinks to sustain our rides. We weren't, in short, stupid. Naive, perhaps!

Clive's leadership role was ever in evidence. A consensus man he likes the team to be 'on board' and harmony is at the heart of his style. It was working. It may be hard to imagine that three, potentially grumpy, old gits, could cohabit for many long days in an ancient van while traversing Europe on cheap bikes, without tension or argument; we did. We were enjoying the focus of navigation, physical hard work and happy exhaustion at the end of each day. We caught and appreciated what we could of the sights and local culture but we were here for cracking mileage and our bodies, so far, had responded well. Clive had been planning this thing for a long while but I never got the sense that his agenda was any other than that of three equal partners pursuing a common goal.

I posted a list of 'key positives so far' after a week of pedalling. We were in Bavaria on the Danube Canal and would soon head into Austria. In a spare moment I wrote: 'People and their welcomes, beauty, cycle-friendliness, mates, laughter, chamois cream, German beer, vineyards, ferrymen, old people on electric bikes, sun, Mothership....'

By contrast - 'Negatives: blocked roads and paths, Duisburg, loadsatraffic, headwinds, green gel, night time disturbances, sleeping with friends (never a good idea), sore bums, Clive's shopping forgetfulness, sharp ceilings in van, all of us losing our specs every hour, toilet arrangements, aching thighs, smelly clothes.... but we're having a ball!'

Talking of smelly clothes, we had had somewhat abortive handwash sessions at a couple of sites. I say abortive because by the time we had pegged out our smalls and malodorous tops and padded lycras, the dew of the evening was settling. Overnight our washing edged slightly from soaking to wet. Thus the Mothership was festooned with damp gear spread throughout the rear cabin in the vain hope that the sun glinting through its windows would dry our soggy gear. Karen Rockell's great SCAD cycling shirts were brilliant adverts for the cause but had the disadvantage of fiercely retaining and intensifying body odour. You know how a curry, kept for several days, becomes ever more aromatic and pungent? You get the message.

Clive took off in the Sunday morning sun (22nd September) from Kelheim to Freinkofen - about 35miles. He posted a video message thanking the BeatSCAD community for their support and, in his PC way, changed his script. 'I'm going to have a cuppa and a bacon sandwich' was vegetarianised so he only got an egg. The times in which we live...

We were now on the Danube proper and majestic it certainly was. We were heading for Aschach an der Donau, about 250 miles from Vienna. Chris's leg took him across the border into Austria. A glorious day for cycling but we needed to crack on because we had a rendezvous in the capital in a couple of days, which we daren't miss. In the evening gloom,

I pedalled over the bridge at Aschach and then down a very long towpath road to the Kaiserhof campsite. What a glorious location at the riverside!

We had made it in time to enjoy a beer and a grand schnitzel meal as befitted our first night in Austria. Having phoned ahead to book a berth for the Mothership, our hosts had kept the kitchen open and treated us quite royally. The pictures posted and my added comments lamented that we couldn't be tourists here and would struggle to keep up to date with the Rugby World Cup. Rain and headwinds were forecast for the morning. The grand surroundings and warm welcome made up for these minor carpings. A large bunch of noisy Italian students parked their tents near the Mothership but even their excitable hubbub didn't stop us dozing off.

Chris headed out of Aschach in early morning drizzle which soon gave way to another bright day, great for cycling. The blue Eurovelo 6 signs were prominent, so too the green Donauweg R1 signs; both were pointing us towards Vienna.

We took a little time out to climb up from the Danube to Mauthausen. It seemed right that we didn't just cycle past this site of persecution without paying our respects. Mauthausen was a Nazi concentration camp about 10 miles east of Linz and on our route to Krems that day. It was a labour camp and part of a large complex of camps, the last to be liberated by the Allies. Greg, Clive's son-in-law's grandfather had survived it. Clive told Antonio's extraordinary story, one of so many. It is worth recording here.

Antonio was an Italian, teenage, anti-fascist, a Partisan, during the Second World War. When his next-door neighbours reported him for anti-fascist activities in 1942, the occupying Nazis arrested and transported him to Mauthausen. In some respects, he was lucky. He had a trade and wasn't put in the hard-labour sector with the Jews. Instead he was pressed into forced labour at the Steyr, Daimler & Puch factory, around 300 metres from the camp, making ball-bearings for Nazi aircraft. Paid in cigarette vouchers, he swapped the vouchers with camp guards for potatoes in order to survive. Of course his fellow Jewish inmates were put to far more punishing work. They had to cope with the 'staircase of death' every day, carrying boulders up a massive stone staircase. Thousands fell by the wayside and died of malnutrition, fatigue or disease.

Antonio survived and eventually was transferred to another forced-labour camp in The Netherlands. It was here, in the midst of the allied invasion, that he was released in September 1944. However, release was as life-threatening as confinement with allied bombings and rogue, retreating Nazis. So, Antonio and many of his fellow prisoners actually stayed in the camp until the American troops arrived to offer some sense of protection.

It was then that he decided to walk home - from The Netherlands to Italy! Sometimes we moan about our situations. In all honesty, we have no idea about stress and deprivation. Because of the allied bombing and the retreating Nazis, he travelled at night and hid by day. Occasionally he would be able to jump onto a train going in vaguely the right direction. Others had a similar idea and Antonio met up with another compatriot who, as it happened, originally lived only 40 kms away from Antonio's home in Italy. They travelled together, scavenging food wherever they could. One night, they secretly took refuge in a German farm which happened to have a pig. They were so desperate that they slaughtered the poor pig with a hammer, shattering Antonio's thumb in the process. With the most rudimentary of cooking facilities - a small fire - they cooked and ate the pig but were so sick that they couldn't move on for three days.

Eventually, having walked most of the way, Antonio jumped on to a final train in Italy heading for his home town. His father, a railway worker at the town's station, literally turned his head in the middle of his shift to see his son climb down from the train. Given that Antonio's parents had no sense of whether he was alive or dead, one can only imagine the overwhelming emotion of that reunion.

The story doesn't end there. Antonio maintained contact with the friend he had made, Giuseppe, and cycled the 40 kms to visit him regularly. On one such visit, he met Giuseppe's sister for the first time. She became Greg's grandmother. Stories like these can only remind us that our lives often hang on the thread of others' fortunes or misfortunes. Antonio's resilience, perhaps good fortune in some respects, and absolute determination to get home; the alignment of the stars which led to Antonio meeting up with Giuseppe. Now Clive's daughter, Amy, has married Antonio's grandson and their son Finley will live to learn of the extraordinary exploits and sufferings of his great grandfather.

Mauthausen is isolated, quiet and forbidding. A moment or two of reflection and then a toast to Antonio.

Back on bikes and on to Krems and the (to us) famous incident of the gas bottle. At the campsite that morning, Clive had been convinced that he had not turned the gas bottle off as part of our MICROBURGERS foolproof checking scheme. He had. When he and Chris wanted to have a cuppa in a supermarket car park while I was doing the middle cycle, no amount of wrist power could turn the bloody thing on. Clive remembers it like this:

> I remember checking the van; we needed the gas to be off for safe travel. I tried to turn anti-clockwise, completely stuck; tried several times, nothing; got a cloth around it, gritted my teeth, nothing. Chris came back from the washing area. He gave it a go, nothing! We had to head off. Late that morning we found, much to Chris's disdain, a service station with a burger bar. Disdain or not, Chris ordered his burger and proceeded to eat...those elements of the burger which he considered nutritious (let's be generous and say half the burger).
>
> Back to the car park for another go at strong arming the gas bottle. No luck, so we thought we'd invite a brawny Austrian couple to have a go. They were a chunky looking pair and he, and even more so his wife or partner, could solve this for sure. He was skinhead, stocky and helpful. She was more brooding - a Brian Moore hooker type. Hence, if I call her a hooker, you know what I mean. Her arms stayed crossed throughout, whilst he, a Duncan Goodhew doppelganger, brought out his best spanner and went for it. Ten minutes later with Duncan much hotter and even more frustrated, he hadn't achieved a millimetre of movement. Gratitude offered and accepted. The female Brian Moore kept her arms across her chest and managed a smile.
>
> When Chris and Paul got to the campsite later in the day some magic happened!

I'll take over the story here. We arrived at the Donaupark Camping Krems site; Clive was on the last leg that day. Chris had told me of the fun and games at the petrol station car park. Over an ale we confided our problem to the campsite barman/factotum. He pulled out a smile and a spanner and headed with us to the Mothership. One look at the gas bottle, nestled in its housing led him to ask whether we were sure which was the right way to turn the bloody thing. Chris looked a tad sheepish. In seconds our man twisted hard counter clockwise and the nut turned. Cue bursts of laughter and an immediate purchase of a large glass of wine for our barman/saviour.

Clive cycled in after a tricky 40 miler to hoots of derision and a shaming in front of our saviour. Clive apologised for making Chris look a polished turd, accepting that he, himself, was the authentic, original gas bottle turd. It's an interesting word but I'm happy that it fits both of them. At least now we were cooking on gas.

Krems has a castle rising above the river and plenty of cafes and bars. We wandered for a while but hunger and fatigue both needed to be satisfied. Tomorrow Vienna beckoned and our ladies would soon be airborne.

8

VIENNA

THE GIRLS: A BREAK FOR TOURISM

Notwithstanding the broad, churning pulse of life that is the Danube, guiding travellers to Vienna's heart, big cities are bloody difficult to cycle into and out of. Roads and cycle paths do not behave as they should, veering off in odd directions and abruptly turning into dead ends or motorways. Vienna has plenty of bridges, docks, underpasses, overpasses; in short, a cyclist's nightmare. It fell to Chris to cycle in to this vast city, boasting eight hundred bridges. Twice as many as Venice, our Lonely Planet Guide explained. Well, which one to meet the hapless Skipper? This wasn't merely a problem of bridges, of course. We had booked an H+ hotel in central Vienna, which unhelpfully had an underground car park with a height restriction. Clive's sleeping compartment would be guillotined if the Mothership tried to break and enter. Few great cities welcome campervans, more's the pity. Clive and I texted Chris to say that we would try for a surface car park near the Reichsbrucke Bridge, along the Handelskai, which flanks the Danube.

We had made fast progress that day to make it to Vienna by mid-afternoon. Amazingly, we found a slot in the Alcoa car park next to the Danube. We rejoiced. Clive spent some time trying to decipher the parking regulations, explained incomprehensibly on giant meters at the entrance barrier. Unsure if we were legal, he hesitatingly paid an extortionate amount for a few hours grace for the Mothership. We had hoped that she could have a two night break in the shadow of the Reichsbrucke but a uniformed parking attendant hove into view. Gloom inevitably descended upon us as he told us that vehicles such as the Mothership were persona non grata. He explained the undesirability of vehicles which looked like traveller hostels. His olive branch was to allow a stay of execution while we grabbed a taxi to our hotel, dumped our stuff and returned to drive the van to the outskirts of town, hopefully to park in some side road free of charge. He insisted that he would pass on knowledge of this agreement to his colleague when he went off duty.

Without labouring the tale, this is what we did. A shiny BMW courtesy of Uber ferried us to and fro, despite the charming but geographically challenged driver being unable to locate our hotel on one of the longest streets in Vienna. No matter, we got there. By the time we returned a fat yellow ticket had been taped to our windscreen. And no parking attendant to plead with. Swear words.

We headed back over the Danube and south east out of the city. Pretty soon we seemed to be in a quieter suburban area on the long Muhlwasser Promenade. Once the ugly signs with tow chains and red verboten crosses disappeared we found a residential side road and we three musketeers pedalled back the three or four miles over the river and through the great Prater Park to find our ladies. All smiles and relief, despite our annoyance at the unforgiving Viennese parking police.

Back at the hotel our irritation further ebbed away as our man at reception confidently advised, "If the ticket is from the government, then you must pay. They will chase. If it's from a private company, ignore. They won't." We ignored.

Chris the skipper (on narrowboats not of the Mothership) is ever on the case of fine food and drink. Sarah Dowdeswell whose sense of style eclipses even that of her husband's (although not the anal elements of it) had booked the hotels for Vienna, Bratislava and Budapest, so we knew that comfort and capital city convenience were assured. Even she didn't know, however, that the most famous craft ale hostelry in town was a two minute wander from our H+ hotel on Liechtensteinstrasse. Chris had already set his ale –divining rods on high alert. We were ready for some fun. The girls were in high spirits. Karen Rockell was ever keen to photograph our every move via her giant iPad. She was to outdo Annie Liebovitz over the next few days and, as she's a teetotaller, all her shots are unaffected by alcoholic twitching.

We needed relaxation and a short time to reflect and be tourists. We were here for two nights. Tomorrow would be a sightseeing indulgence. Back home the big news story was the collapse of Thomas Cook. Thousands of holidaymakers were either trying to get repatriated or were sitting at home airports frustrated that their travel had been scuppered. Jeremy Corbyn was again in the headlines for sitting on the fence over Brexit. His star was waning fast and only in his 'Momentum' bubble was there any more than a glimmer of hope for him. As we quaffed our flight of taster ales in The Beaver Brewing Co., the girls brought the news from home and we planned our next moves. I kept a record of the beers - or rather a photo of the ale list. It reads like a Michelin Star menu. Blue Sky, Scarecrow, High 5, Lincoln Duncan,

Vindobona, Great Lakes, Holiday and Coopers were beers lovingly and intensely described. Our favourite (after tasting six) was Red Molly: a rich and luscious red ale featuring citrus notes and an extensive spectrum of malt, hops etc. At 5.4% it was going to start our evening off well. Later we would stumble into an exceptional Thai (?) restaurant not far from our hotel and enjoy a vast meal at surprisingly limited cost. I have a photograph of Chris and Karen sitting under a large chalkboard menu with the banner headline MUCK e FUCK. None of us had any idea what this meant but it makes a great photo....and tastes good with rice!

I had visited Vienna a couple of years earlier with my old schoolfriend Terry Charman. He was a senior and celebrated historian at the Imperial War Museum. Very sadly he had died earlier in the year having stoically fought cancer for some time. Terry knew Vienna well and his extraordinary historical knowledge allowed him authoritative and waspish comments on almost every aspect of Viennese life. He had taken me to bars and cafes, museums and galleries that I would never have sought out for myself. Each of his choices was especially selected. We had stayed at the Maria Theresa hotel. "Paul, I like this place. I feel at home for a couple of reasons. Firstly Maria Theresa was the only female Hapsburg to rule pretty much half of Europe and she was the mother of Marie Antoinette. More importantly they serve cocktails until 2am."

We had wandered down a rather grubby backstreet and into a dark alehouse and Terry said, "Hitler used to love this little bar you know. He would sit on a stool by the kitchen so he could pat the waitresses on their bums when they emerged." Unpleasant but the least of his excesses. Later in the day he had had some work to do in the Arsenal, the Viennese equivalent of the Imperial War Museum. To see the car in which Archduke Franz Ferdinand was travelling when he was shot in Sarajevo and, further, to see the bloodstained tunic on display was a riveting experience. The trigger of the First World War. I had caught up with Terry as I was wandering through the section on the upheavals of the 1930s, the Anschluss and the Second World War. "Don't spend too long reading the blurb on the exhibits. The Austrians are pretty economical with the truth." He had guffawed with laughter. What a great guide and lovely, encyclopaedically knowledgeable man he was.

The girls and boys took tourist buses and wandered through the grand streets of the city. The Schonbrunn Palace and gardens were a vast delight. Quite a lot of Vienna is vast and the imperial and imperious buildings rise up regularly in one's eyeline as reminders of the dynastic ambitions of the Hapsburgs and the monuments built to celebrate themselves. Now in July 2020, as we currently ponder the validity of monuments which may reflect a questionable past, I wonder whether this trend will find similar favour in countries and cultures who prefer an alternative zeitgeist?

Back at the Palace we all sat down to the most expensive coffee and cakes in Europe at the Cafe Concerto. At least Karen got some stunning shots of us enjoying being fleeced. The views were almost worth it. Whistle-stop tours and city breaks are marvellous but the great metropolises of the world have a similar cultural ambition - visitor attraction. This is not to say that Vienna with its schnitzel and cake, its waltzing and Riding School and the great wheel of the Prater reminding us of Orson Welles and the Third Man, hasn't got cultural definition. However we had already caught some of the realities of rural and more remote areas - and there was a great deal more ahead. There is a great sense of connectedness and affluence in world cities. Shortly we would be venturing into the unvisited and unloved villages of remote eastern Europe where economic deprivation and tribal identity dominate the prevailing atmosphere.

9
GIRLS ON BIKES
BLYTON'S CHILDREN HEAD FOR
BRATISLAVA AND BEYOND

Thursday 26th September. Chris and Sarah headed off to pick up the hire bike while Clive and I cycled to pick up the Mothership. The former excursion was more successful than the latter. Having cycled through the Prater only 24 hours earlier, Clive and I and Google maps failed miserably in retracing our steps. Nor did any of the pleasant Viennese strollers show much recognition of their own city as they struggled to help us find Muhlwasserstrasse, the site of the stranded Mothership. Well, we got there eventually and returned to find Chris and Sarah fully togged up and ready for action. Our plan was for each couple to take a chunk of the mileage. Slovakia being Austria's neighbour and the two capitals being only 50 miles apart, the day was going to be a doddle. Well, actually, it was. Despite Chris blaming a Viennese Irishman for misdirecting on the outskirts of Vienna, which led to a five mile detour around a cement works, all went smoothly. Sarah, being quite used to her husband's shows of overconfidence, showed neither sympathy nor surprise at their minor detour. Perhaps mild irritation.

Clive and Karen took the second leg. Karen powered off in the lead - a position she held throughout their stint. Given her new liver, her repaired heart and the daily diet of drugs to keep her alive, her power on the pedals was a marvel. Belinda and I took over for the run into Bratislava. We cycled over the Danube on the Novy Most - New Bridge, which is next to Stary Most - Old Bridge. The advantage of the new one is that it has a separate cycle path. Great joy. Less joy was the palaver of getting on to it through carrying our bikes up a great flight of access steps. Sarah had, once again, booked us into a comfortable auberge, The Radisson Park Inn no less! Advantages of this place included the short walk into the old city, the river views, the spacious bar and a car park fit for our Mothership.

We had time to wander the buzzing old town, full of cafes and bars. Attractive and friendly, like so many other European hubs, it was hard to place this small capital city in a wider context. Bordered by Poland in the north, then clockwise, Ukraine, Hungary, Austria and the Czech Republic, it's a mountainous country and we were passing along the flat bit - the Danube valley. Having separated from Czechoslovakia in 1993 in what was dubbed the Velvet Divorce, Slovakia seems to have become an affluent member of the EU (from 2004) and the Eurozone. Its history, like so much of central and eastern Europe, is littered with power struggles. The Ottomans, the Hapsburgs and the Magyars all fought for ultimate influence before the twentieth century, when Hitler took a hand. The muscle flexing of various Goliaths over the Davids of central Europe and the Balkans is not something that your average Brit thinks about much. After 1066 and all that we have had some internal strife from time to time but little to compare perhaps with the political and tribal upheavals that each of these nations has experienced in the distant and, indeed, recent past.

Clive and Karen took to the bikes the following morning. We were hopping into Hungary and making for Gyor, some 60 miles away. Belinda and I took over and made good progress to Hedervar a small village boasting a church and a football-themed bar with the scarves of numerous European superclubs lining its walls. Our lunch was memorable for Karen's chair collapsing and Chris and Sarah each cycling off in different directions having agreed which way to go.

Well, they managed to get their act together and arrived, late afternoon in Gyor. This is a small and charming riverside town with a cobbled and pedestrianised centre. There is a London Eye lookalike which similarly dominates the south bank of the Danube. Our hotel was tucked away up a small side street but access to the centre was prevented by large electrically operated bollards which raised and fell when buses neared but didn't seem to be very friendly otherwise. We discovered that by speaking into a roadside telephone we could plead for access by confirming our business. And so, magically, a bollard descended for just long enough for the Mothership to glide into the old town centre. Chris and Sarah pedalled in over the cobbles. While we wandered around in the early evening, there were frantic preparations for a rock concert and party on the riverside under the wheel. There was fun and frivolity in the air as Belinda and I wandered the cobbles, idly checking our cycling route out of town the following day. An extraordinary bang and scraping stopped us in our tracks. We turned to see a boy racer's car impaled on the stump of an electric bollard. His frantic reversing off the thing only served to make the damage far worse. The Mothership had enjoyed a far more serene trip across into the town centre.

The sound of the riverside celebrations can be heard on the posted video. We had drinks in a street bar and moved on to the brilliant Kisfaludy Gourmet Wine Bar and Restaurant. Sounds grand but it was an intimate and atmospheric bistro run by a husband and wife team who loved their work. The video doesn't quite capture the charm but it was all chalkboards, wine bottles and lovely aromas blending with the conversational hubbub. Our host chatted with passion about his business. Bliss. I was moved to post a blog late that night.

As you leave the crisp efficiency of Germany and Austria, it is noticeable that the economic well-being begins to shift into a lower gear. Slovakia, charming and attractive, has its infrastructure projects snailing along. Where the EU puts its weight behind things - such as our bike path - the progress seems admirable. Here and, today in Hungary the road surfaces deteriorate into a condition recognised as UK pothole syndrome.

The Slavonic body type and physiognomy is quickly replaced by the Magyar stockiness and punishing jawline. From Bratislava to Gyor the change is seen in just a few miles. Both these places have charming cobbled, pedestrianised centres and turbulent histories which belie the friendly charm of cafe banter. In Gyor their 'London Eye' was being opened on the banks of the Danube. Tina Turner and Abba covers were blaring from the riverside tribute band. The streets thronged with the young - our group were the oldest swingers in town. Our meal at the rightly renowned Kisfaludy restaurant was a highlight. We are carboloading for the hundreds of miles ahead as we travel east and south towards Istanbul.

The Hungarian Forint goes much further than the euro of the last couple of weeks. A beer is £1. We haven't seen much ethnic diversity at all. White is the primary colour, here in Hungary and in Slovakia. Indeed in Vienna too. London seems so much more ethnically diverse from where we stand on the Danube. We are all pondering on matters at home as we travel across the continent which, to some extent, the UK has rejected. OK that's a bit over the top but you know what I mean. As I type with my EU tee-shirt on, our group has felt the Eurolove to a considerable degree so far.

The girls are nearing the end of their stay with us but we have had a blast with a combination of modest cycling and tourist indulgence. Visegrad tomorrow, about 80 miles and a short pedal into Budapest the day after. Then the boys crack on into Serbia and Romania, Bulgaria and Turkey, while the girls fly off, hopefully to return when we reach the Blue Mosque.

We much enjoyed our time in Gyor but with 80 plus miles for the six of us to negotiate the following day on our journey to Visegrad, moving on was in our thoughts. With the girls sharing a bike which had been set up so that it suited (more or less) all three, we could have no overlap of cycling legs. One couple came into a meeting point and the next couple took over. No overlaps and therefore no time to lose. The girls were fit and ready for the challenge. All systems go.

10
VISEGRAD AND BUDAPEST
AND GOODBYE GIRLS

Clive was checking our BeatSCAD totals regularly and with Karen, our SCAD survivor with us, it was rather more in our thoughts. We kept being delighted by the gradual ticking up of the numbers. By Gyor we had moved up to £3500. Karen is a trustee of the Charity and spends a good deal of her time working for and promoting the cause. It goes without saying that small charities which try so hard to publicise and fund barely known afflictions such as SCAD, have uphill struggles. Karen made sure that our wander across Europe was getting as much public oxygen as she could muster.

Of course the main contributors were always going to be friends and family but they rose to the occasion in great number. Our sporting connections piled in as well. High fives to them all. (Did I really type that?)

From Gyor the Danube meanders gently south east towards Budapest. We had planned to stay only 40 miles outside the Hungarian capital - at Visegrad where the river turns sharply south. This small town boasts a mediaeval citadel and an early Renaissance summer palace of King Matthias Corvinus of Hungary. This meant little to Belinda and me as we pedalled out of Gyor.

Chris and Sarah rather enjoyed cycling through Esztergom, a mediaeval town with an ancient bridge across the Danube to link with Slovakia. Each couple had less than a thirty mile stint with Clive and Karen taking the anchor leg. We spotted them cycling happily past the hotel so a quick phone call rescued them from pedalling on into the town and getting hopelessly lost or at least late for supper.

I took to my diary blog again that night.

It was 80 miles today from Gyor to Visegrad. Travelling eastwards we travel back in time. Nagyszentjanos, Bana Babolna, Dunaalmas, Neszmely, Sutto, Labatlan, Nyergesufalu, Tat, Acs, Komarom, Esztergom and Pilismarot were amongst the villages and towns we careered through before arriving late afternoon in Visegrad. Esztergom was the capital of Hungary from around the 10th to 13th centuries. Then King Bela IV moved his royal posterior to Buda.

Along the northern side of Hungary the Magyars look across the Danube at the Slovaks. The fortifications of Esztergom bear witness to border feuding of old. The default setting for the stern, unsmiling Magyar is cup-half-empty. We stopped at roadside cafes to stony welcomes which only warmed when we smiled and paid and, unlike others, returned our coffee cups like good little boys. The locals having cheap beers on a Saturday lunchtime seemed grudging in their recognition of foreign travellers: not hostile but watchful.

Moving out of Gyor we were in to a shabbier world almost immediately. Gone were the shiny Mercs of the Viennese streets, replaced by an assortment of elderly vehicles: Suzukis, Fords, Skodas, Audis, Renaults. Battered and bruised mostly. The rural economy was at once charming and hard, very hard. We saw many smallholdings, grapes being harvested, pumpkins aplenty and each village had harvest effigies like guys stacked at the village sign to signal the business of the community.

The men in the bars had an air of the gulag about them. Too strong? Well the Magyar originated in the Urals and made his way down in the 9th century. Today over 90% of the 10 million Hungarians share this heritage and the larger proportion is Catholic.

Their entry into the EU in 2004 must be a godsend. The increase of factories, cement works, refineries and quarries on the edges of towns speaks of a slowly evolving economy. And yet the main characteristic we could pick out was a dourness which seems inherited from the privations of previous generations. Nonetheless the major roads are being upgraded fast.

Villages have their central roads and pathways spruced up. On all minor roads the surfaces are appalling. This is, presumably, the EU's phase 2 for bringing Magyardom up to speed. And perhaps leaving behind those Ural frowns.

However, the Hungarian Forint languishes somewhat and while the locals find it hard to show their teeth in a grin, the mention of Ferenc Puskas can transform you from being a nosey outsider into one of the chaps who understands at least one of the heroes of Hungary. Sport remains a lifesaver.

So another lovely autumn day and an extraordinary spa hotel that Mrs Dowdeswell had booked us into - Hotel Therm! This grand but austere edifice sat on a hillside outside the town. Bubbling jacuzzis and a huge heated pool ran outside along the length of the hotel. Wealthy looking Hungarians were padding around in towelling dressing gowns in the foyer. We learned that this place was a conference centre for central European politicians. It had the air of a Communist Party luxury hideaway, not that I have any idea what that might be like. Certainly, despite its current opulence, there was the architecture and brutality of what used to be called the Eastern Bloc. It is a truth, universally acknowledged, that socialists and communists rail against the privilege of the capitalist toffs but love a little pampering themselves given half a chance.

I am reminded of my elder brother's 70th birthday party. Bear with me. He had a big bash at the plush Grand Hotel in Brighton, February 2020, just before Lockdown. The Labour Party hustings were being held there; Keir Starmer, Lisa Nandy and the, now, recently sacked Rebecca Long-Bailey were padding round this vastly expensive setting, surrounded by Momentum groupies, old Labour and New Labour luvvies. Champers and finger-food fun. Hardly street food in Camden Market, nor fish and chips on Scarborough seafront. Anyway, back to the story.

We didn't need the spa pampering but were pleased that a Casablanca style pianist was entertaining guests in the bar. Chris was appalled at the poor selection of ales but we all perked up at the quality of the vast buffet in the great dining hall. As with so many hotels, you think that there are few punters in residence and then, when the dinner gong goes, a football crowd seeps out of the woodwork. We got into conversation with a Hungarian (well he would be I suppose) and his English wife. They were on a weekend break from Budapest. She was a teacher who had lived in Hungary for nearly twenty years. While she liked the buzz of Budapest she lamented the corruption of politicians and other officials.

"We have been a member of the EU for fifteen years but, outside the cities there is little change. EU money is wasted or stolen." Quite a blunt assessment, I felt, given that I am a fan of the European Project. "Not all countries have leaders to be proud of," she added. Well she can say that again.

As I write now in July 2020, Leicester has been locked down and a little lad called Tony Hudgell, a five year old double amputee, has raised over £1million for the local hospital which saved his life. The abuse he had suffered as a baby by his birth parents resulted in the appalling injuries from which he miraculously survived. Now adopted by wonderful parents and inspired by Captain Tom, now Sir Tom, Tony has walked twelve kilometres on his new prosthetics for the institution which saved him. As I switch from being in the midst of the most profound period of national crisis of my lifetime to our happy story of a trans-European adventure of just a few months ago, the uplifting acts of heroism and simple humanity seem to affect me disproportionately. The bitter arguments of Brexit have been replaced by the febrile intensity of government failings, the civil unrest provoked by the Black Lives Matter campaign and the Covid carelessness of thousands of plain stupid Brits who want to party on a Bournemouth beach or rave in Manchester. The nation's apparent desperation to lie prostrate and inebriated on a boiling beach on the Costa del Sol is high on our Government's list of priorities - aka getting tourism and the aircraft industry back up and running. I should acknowledge the very high level of compliance, generally, with lockdown rules. The scenes of mass breakout, so eagerly sought by salivating media, have been relatively rare. As I type Jofra Archer has been suspended from the England cricket team for breaking the strict rules of the Test match 'bio-bubble'. He won't do that again.

Such a scenario could hardly be dreamed of as Chris and Sarah set off for the first of three short stints which would take us into Budapest on the Sunday morning of September 29th. Belinda and I cycled in through the Buda part of town, along the Danube with the majestic parliament buildings and St. Stephen's Basilica welcoming us in sunshine on the far bank. We cycled over the famous old chain bridge, the Szechenyi Lanchid and made our way through the winding cobbled streets of the old town to a small, dark bicycle shop. We peered in. This was the last stop for the girls' hire bike which had served them so well in three countries. We ventured a cautious *Hello, is anyone here?* From beneath a counter a girl who appeared to be about 14 jumped up and, in the disarmingly open and confident way that travelling American students have, sang out *Hiya, I'm Alice, you gotta bike for me?* Indeed we had and we got her life story in return. A typical brave, brash, smiling Californian, who was taking life by the scruff of the neck, even though working in the bike shop could be a tad tedious at times.

Now it is quite something to pick up a bike in one country and drop it off a couple off nations down the road. Brilliant work by Sarah Dowdeswell to seek out and nail the multinational bike hire! More praise was due for booking us into the small Ibis Styles hotel on the Rakoczi Ut, a long boulevard running from the centre of the city. A helpful concierge saved a space for the Mothership immediately outside the front door. Never has an ancient campervan enjoyed a more privileged overnight stay. Budapest central. Our bikes were safely chained to a hot water pipe to which the attendant gruffly directed us in the underground car park.

We had a little time to explore for we had booked two nights. I guess this was for the girls to enjoy more of their mini-break. We boys were pleased to spend time with our spouses but the niggling thought of another fifteen hundred miles (2400kilometres sounds worse) was in our minds. We had lost a little focus in the ease and enjoyment of the last few days but we knew what was ahead. The only thing to do was go for a beer.

Late afternoon, Chris set his iPhone to beer divining mode and strode down the Rakoczi Ut, then twisted this way and that in search of a beery paradise. He found an extraordinary bazaar-like indoor market, thronging with bars and food and people and music and buzz. A souk Budapest-style. With excellent beer. Later Chris told me that these bars are called Ruin Pubs. Make of that what you will.

Clive had found an Indian restaurant and a launderette. Weird how one craves a Chicken Jalfrezi in a central European city but we had done with schnitzels and goulash and knew that plenty of fatty pork awaited in Serbia and Romania. In the event the restaurant only took cash and our Hungarian Florints were in short supply.

On the brighter side Clive arranged for his smalls to be service washed the following day. In the end we opted for a sheltered table outside in the early evening sunshine and managed another worthy Hungarian repast.

We had a fine whistle stop tour of the main sights the next day. We metro-ed to the waterfront and took in the magnificent Hungarian Parliament which, with the Danube, provides a spectacular setting for the Memorial of the Shoes. This poignant sculpture of sixty pairs of iron shoes attached to the stone embankment, serves to give remembrance of the Jews and many others who were ordered to take off their shoes and were shot at the edge of the water by the Arrow Cross Party, their bodies falling into the Danube.

From this moving tribute we moved on across the old chain bridge and up to Buda Castle on the vertiginous funicular, the Budavari Siklo. We caught the very formal changing of the guard at the Castle gates and then Sorensens and Dowdeswells succumbed to the lure of ale and chips in a lovely hill top terrace overlooking the land beyond the city. Clive and Karen headed back to the launderette for some bathos and clean undies. Look it up.

By the evening the boys were getting twitchy. Chris observed that he felt that he had gone a bit soft. Well that's what a kiss and a cuddle with your wife does for you. Or, as Clive said, sex. Whatever the case Clive was keen to get in the saddle by 6.30 the next morning. Our track record of struggling to find the right route out of major cities caused some nervousness. Grudgingly we all got up for an early breakfast to wave our leader off. The girls had plenty of time to get their act together for a lunchtime flight back home. Karen would take back the news of our breaking £4000 to the SCAD community and albums-full of photographs. The ladies had been great support and fun. Time to crack on.

Chris and I loaded up our refreshed Mothership and headed out of town. We drove to Domsod, some 40miles due south. My leg was next - to Uszod, a similar distance and Chris would cycle into Baja that evening. The campsite, cheap as chips was on the edge of this attractive little town which nestled on a tributary of the Danube. The site was all but deserted but the showers worked and pleasing noises and smells were emanating from an apparently jolly Hungarian cafe nearby. Our host was all bonhomie, his wife Cruella de Ville. "Do you take cards?" "Yes," he said, "No," she countermanded. "Euros?" Same response. Chris recalls it similarly.

Yes, a riverside campsite with lots of mossies. Met for the first time the husband of Scottish couple who had the very tiny tent. Turns out they are cycling to Cape Town. My ride was dominated by long views to the Great Hungarian plain to the north and the paprika fields, and riparian woodland that blocked out the Danube for most of the ride - good word, eh? Clive, you must recall our evening meal when we voted that you go off to find a cash point to pay for Paul and my quite delicious chilli meal. Table service disagreeable to say the least.

11

TO BACKA PALANKA, SERBIA VIA CROATIA

Tuesday. Backa Palanka is a grubby and unattractive town which is half in Croatia and half in Serbia. The Danube provides the border for much of the division between these two states. We had to get out of Hungary first. The river continues its winding route south and I followed but had to grab a ferry at Mohacs to follow the Eurovelo path. Another sparkling day. The Mohacs ferry on video reminds me again of the hundreds of such small ferries which cross the great rivers of Europe every few minutes, back and forth all day long. A Euro, a few Forints, a Dinar or two. I pedalled out of Hungary but there was considerable border scrutiny. With some glee I sped past the queue in which the Mothership sat and waited in Croatia in a lay-by for the boys to catch up.

Clive was to be grateful more than once for doing a belt and braces job on his paperwork. His attaché case, often mislaid, of course, was filled with documents, some of which had very tenuous connections to the trip. However, central and east European jobsworths on border posts tend to conform to type: unsmiling, unbending, ungrateful for your presence in their country. The welcome signs we see when entering someone else's country are not endorsed by the border and customs officials who guard the entrance and exit routes. Of course Clive needed to show Mothership registration documents and insurance certificates. He probably had his birth certificate and inside leg measurements somewhere in the attaché case. We each carried a little money and passports with us when we were cycling. Until Clive forgot to do this after we crossed into Romania. A story to tell later.

Croatia, like all the Balkan countries, has been kicked about by various bullies but emerged after the Second World War as Yugoslavia. This hotchpotch of republics were uneasy bedfellows and remain so: Croats, Serbs, Slovenes, Montenegrins, Macedonians and Bosnians. Things fell apart - the centre could not hold. Croatia became independent in 1991 and a member of the EU in 2013. We get the impression from the tourism, the sailing and the islands that Croatia is affluent. We saw little of that. Much of the country has a poor, rural economy.

Chris took over from me and arrived in a small village, Dalj, hot and sweaty. Meanwhile Clive and I had to take the Mothership across open fields, as directed by diversion signs. We queried heading off through wheat fields with a local but, with only his nodding head to guide us, he insisted that we drive into farmland. Google maps, hilariously went haywire as it kept trying to reconfigure the impossible. A Facebook video humorously has a Google girl getting very confused as we turn against her guiding suggestions. We got to Dalj, by hook or crook and the Mothership enjoyed her miles off-road.

If there was one thing you couldn't forget on a day like today, it was hydration. Well blow me down if Clive didn't set off on the last leg into Backa Palanka, without any water at all. After a few minutes I got an SOS call in the Mothership. Little I could do until Chris arrived and he was struggling with the heat and headwinds. Clive soldiered on. Indeed he soldiered on in his ageing stupidity, for 35 miles, without a drink. Madness, but he survived. When Chris arrived he regaled me with his experience in a remote village shop when he stopped for a rest.

I loved my ride through the Croatian vineyards on a gorgeous day. Not so the "road from hell" towards the Serbian border out of Osijek. Stopped to buy a drink in a tiny village, proffered 9 Euros for a bitter lemon - thought it a bit expensive - lady eventually able to explain that Croatia was not in the Euro. Hadn't thought I might need some Kuna. Never mind. I think we agreed on a couple of Euros. Very hot, very thirsty day and couldn't wait to get to our luxury accommo in BP. Came across Scots couple again in BP, out of water. Very attractive wife with a nice pair of pins, mid-twenties. So, I offered to accompany her to my luxury quarters to fill her bottles. As you do. Off they then went to wild camp. Madness. Less said about the hostel the better. Photo evidence says it all.

The hostel to which Chris alluded was a sub Maze prison affair at a crossroads in the middle of town. Clive had secured a dormitory for the three of us via a dodgy phone call while aboard the Mothership south of Budapest. Chris and I arrived, having given water to a dehydrated party leader and left him to cycle into Backa. A swarthy man appeared and told us that we were late. He made us hang around in a rather cloak and dagger fashion while he located keys. Clearly he wanted to bugger off for the evening and leave us to it. The prison we were kipping down in, had a series of locked doors with weighty mortices to secure you as you went through each pod. We had to unlock and lock behind us as we went. There were locks on the showers, the toilet block and every door leading into the corridors on each of four or five storeys. We locked our bikes in the basement. Our dorm was on the third floor. Lock, unlock, lock, unlock...and into our three bedded cell.

This was a hostel for itinerant workers. Smells of booze and fags and one or two other things. Gruff voices. Keep your doors locked and your money and passport tight. Every street seemed to have a miniscule time limit on parking. We tried to make payment via phone but far too much was lost in translation so we gave in to fatigue and the need for a bath, secured by multiple padlocks. We parked outside the front door and prepared to take what came. Again, at some point later, we were to pay for this cavalier approach.

The rain settled in for the evening and we made our way out for food. We found no restaurants but stumbled into a bar...of course. As we remarked on the dearth of eateries our young barman told us that there was a vast and excellent restaurant next door; we must have walked past it! Indeed it was vast and excellent. A tricky day had ended well...almost. Chris spotted an ATM and wanted a few Serbian Dinars to see us into Romania. Confused by beer and stupidity he managed to extract £250 worth, rather than the intended £25. Easy mistake to make. He was now hell-bent on spending cash for petrol, groceries, B&Bs and campsites, the lot. Clive and I were keen that he took plenty of useless dinars back to Blighty to sit in his desk at home as a reminder of his inability to count.

The night heralded an explosion of thunder and lightning. By morning the rain was still pelting down. Naturally we picked the parking ticket off the windscreen. Clive left his padded shorts in the room. We weren't surprised.

12

CAMP DUNAV: OUTSKIRTS OF BELGRADE

We drove a mile or so out of town in a downpour and breakfasted in Celarevo, waiting for the rain to ease. Chris saw a chink of blue in the weighty dark cumulus overhead and ventured out. We had reckoned on 90 miles to Zemun, just outside Belgrade. Chris sent me his diary note 'take' on the start of the day.

> Very wet that morning so skip reluctant to ride immediately but was kicked out of the van a couple of miles out of BP and told to get a grip. Quite right too.

I made the campsite, Camp Dunav, first while Chris and Clive were trying to get rid of some Dinars in a petrol station and supermarket. There was a charming welcome committee, including a sturdy Serbian girl with military bearing and brutal English. I took rather a shine to her since she promised that she would open the beer fridge when our Dinars arrived. The few campers about seemed keen to chat.

After a while I jotted some notes.

It's strange what things occupy one's thoughts on a marathon like this. The quality of toilets and showers on remote campsites; why are Tesco all over Hungary but nowhere else? Do we need chamois cream if the weather is cold? Can we get rid of our Hungarian Forints before we get to Serbia? As for Serbian Dinar, how can we spend enough of it when Chris had an ATM brainstorm and took out ten times more than was required.

Our preoccupations tumble forth. When on the bikes - usually between four and five hours each per day, we fix ourselves into a focused mindset and, simply, plough on. This is difficult when we see the bullet-ravaged buildings of the border towns of Croatia and Serbia, staring at their erstwhile enemies across the Danube divide. As we left Backa Palanka this morning the vast cemetery which stretches for several hundred metres on the road to Belgrade, presents a sobering vista of thousands of graves, unsettlingly marked by newly-masoned dark granite.

Whatever impressions, some cheaply made, about the locals as we pass through must be informed by the troubles - all too recent- of this turbulent area of Europe, the Balkans.

It is intriguing to see the hold-ups at borders where the EU has yet to smooth passenger and freight transport through. The goods vehicles suffer the most. Brexit beware. These troubled nations of Serbia, Hungary and Bulgaria have a way to go before their infrastructure can heave them up (their cities apart) to an acceptable standard of living for this day and age. We in the Mothership wonder if the possible downturn in our economy and the stifling of business and trade will see our well-being, economically and socially, take a real hit.

We focus on the day to day and try to enjoy the physical challenge as well as observing and interacting as much as possible with the changing environment and the friendly people whom we have encountered. Serbia seems full of people who can stumble through quite adequately in English. God knows how they have managed this.

Today I have been guided by a woman walking up a country lane carrying two heavy bags and the campsite receptionist spoke near-perfect English; our companions on the banks of the Danube outside Belgrade tonight are German, Dutch and Serbian. The former two are baffled by Brexit but hold the British in high esteem. For now, I guess.

Later I added:

> Camp Dunav is in Zemun, a large suburb of Belgrade. The name seems improbable for a campsite; rather it has echoes of Mash or Alan Sherman's Hallo Mudder. And our Serbian hosts found the three old men on bikes as amusing as both those classics.
>
> Amongst the hardy group of travellers at the Camp, was a formidable woman who announced herself as 'The big fat German lady'. With a grand command of English and a fierce intelligence this fifty-something madam was a sight (and sound) to behold. She drove a camper van similar to the Mothership and was touring the Balkans to 'remind myself of the curious and complicated geopolitical quandaries of the area.' Wow. When I told her of our adventure her response was a hearty, if sneering, 'Mad dogs and Englishmen!' She then linked our

stupidity with Brexit. On the whole, though, she liked the people of the UK. 'They can laugh at themselves; others think they can but the English do it the best.' Hard not to warm to this large lady. She told me the story of taking her prize dog to a show in Edinburgh last year. She had driven from Dusseldorf. The dog show was in a conference centre near Edinburgh airport. Her pooch hates aircraft noise. Disaster darling. She turned her camper van round and drove home. She was well-versed in Anglo Saxon expletives. With some relish she told me that she was a 'Schpeenster'. No man would dare tell her what to do. I certainly wouldn't.

Clive's take on the experience was more to the point.

Campsite with overweight but strangely alluring campsite owner? Paul making cultural contact with 'Miss Whiplash' strident German woman, indicating in ways which none of us would dare to disagree that the British were 'completely stupid' to leave the EU...or words to that effect.

In the brief time we were at Camp Dunav, we took to calling it the Gulag, somewhat uncharitably. The Serbs had treated us very well and were to continue to do so. Whereas the somatotype of the male Hungarian could be classed as a cross between Fred Flintstone and a sumo wrestler, your average Serb seemed more a Novak Djokovic clone.

Infrastructure projects, particularly great swathes of concrete punching through and around towns and villages, are evident. So too the potholes and tough roads which plague Serbia and Hungary; less so Croatia. We complain about the UK but Serbian craters top any tarmac psoriasis that dear old Blighty serves up.

And the speed of cars and jugger-buggers as they career down these mottled highways has to be seen to be believed. Of course Big Brother is less apparent than in the ubiquitous closed circuitry of our homeland. Speed cameras are a rarity and police, surprisingly, seem to take a low profile away from the towns.

Not so the border guards. As we flit in and out of the EU or Schengen zones the jobsworths delight in the steely grab of the passport. It's the same the world over. A final Jelen beer from the camp commandant saw us turn in for the night with plenty of mileage beyond Belgrade for us to tackle in the morning.

13
TO THE IRON GATES OF SERBIA
AND MAMA MILA

Clive set off at 7am to negotiate Belgrade and the first 45 miles to Skorenovac. It was a pity that we didn't have time to check out the Serbian capital. Of huge strategic importance in the Balkans, the city, being Yugoslavia's former capital, has been kicked around between the Romans, Byzantines, Bulgars, Hungarians, Ottomans and Hapsburgs to name a few. The Serbs, Slavs, Slovenes and Croats, recently lumped together are now apart. Belgrade sits at the confluence of the Strava and Danube. The stories this city could tell. I need to return and check it out properly. I probably won't revisit Camp Dunav, but you never know.

I took over for the next leg to Stara Palanka, a ferry point across the Danube. I had some rough ground to cover and I was glad of the shock absorption on my front forks. After Belgrade the Danube turns east again as it cuts across to Romania. We were in pretty wild country and heading for the famous Iron Gates Gorge on the Danube. Before that, on the rough ground of the northern shore I was cycling alone. I hadn't seen anyone for half an hour. I saw, ahead of me, a group of three or four mangy dogs picking over what I took to be the carcasses of birds or rabbits or the like. One raised its head as, I guess, my scent floated downwind. Immediately the dogs raced after me, the lead creature snarling and yapping at my legs. He got a good bite on my trainers and I was pleased that I wasn't wearing some thin designer cycle shoe. I had thick, hefty trainers and I screamed at the rabid pack to bugger off. Out of nowhere a tramp-like figure rose from a recumbent position in thick grass and yelled something impressive in Serbian and the dogs scattered. I pedalled on frantically.

In Serbia, Romania and northern Bulgaria we saw many dogs roaming the streets and fields, scavenging alone and in packs. Some seemed wild, others belonged but were left to roam free. We invariably picked up speed when one or more hove into view. In the more remote areas, yards and compounds were guarded by chained Alsatians who ran to the limit of tethering to snarl and scream-bark as we cycled by. It was hard not to be intimidated. Wild boar roamed the wastes of farmland and roadside signs warned off travellers from stopping too long and eating food. We neither saw any wild boar nor did we linger at the roadside.

Chris had already set off from the strange ferry point at Stara Palanka, aiming along the south side of the Danube for a campsite at Dobra. Clive was there with the Mothership. Clive and I caught a later ferry - an extraordinary crossing where the ramp that took the Mothership on to the landing craft had to be made safe by a good deal of spade and shingle work by the ferrymen. The boat was a D-Day landing craft and the pilot a jovial chappie who understood not one word of what we said. The experience was mutual and warm.

The light was fading fast behind the deep gorges of the eastern Danube. We couldn't find a campsite open. Chris, ahead on his bike, had done a great stint and needed beer and shower and food and bed. As we were preparing for a night at the roadside in the Mothership, Dobra, a tiny lakeside hamlet, served up a small guest house. Dragan a genial young host and his mother Mama Mila, opened their arms and made their house ours. Soup and belly-pork stew and walnut cake and beer. Bed and bath and brekki the next day which looked strikingly similar to the 90% fat content of last night's meal. It's a wonder that more Serbs don't drop dead of heart attacks after they leave school.

Mama Mila, a woman whose age was anything from fifty to ninety, was all beaming smiles and finger wagging when we pushed large lumps of fat to the sides of our plates. Dragan, her son, dutifully fetched the food and beer and seemed genuinely delighted to have found some stray punters looking for beds. When it came to payment Mama Mila eyed Chris's brimming wallet and helped herself. £16 each for B,B and evening meal...and beer. Cheap as chips.

They waved us off from the tiny hamlet that is their remote home. The photos of the imposing Dragan and his diminutive but equally imposing Mama Mila, will always serve to remind us of Serbian hospitality.

The Iron Gates is a giant gorge on the Danube separating Serbia from Romania. Along the stretch of gorge there are numerous tunnels ranging from 100 to 800 metres. They are dark and unlit but cycling along the fast and relatively quiet main road and zipping through the tunnels was exhilarating. When you emerge from the darkness of a tunnel the rocks rise high above you to south and north, bisected by the Danube coursing through the valley. Chris took over from me to negotiate the vast bridge and border crossing at Drobeta-Turnu Severin that would take us into Romania. Again Clive's attaché case came to our rescue as he provided this and that for customs and border police. The queue at the border was greater than the traffic on the road might have suggested. However we were now moving from non-EU Serbia back into the EU.

Chris observed later that Serbia had seemed quite affluent. He had spotted a number of Chinese wandering around building sites. We speculated that China and even Russia might be investing hard in this curious country with a reputation for back-door deals. But what do we know?

14
AN EXPERIENCE WITH VERONIKA

Chris had a tricky leg that lunchtime. He negotiated the last of the Iron Gates and had a long haul across the Danube border into Romania to meet me shortly afterwards. He recalled the increasing problems which our road routes were to pose.

Some big hills along the Iron Gates, and dangerous road into Drobeta - a real taste of the Balkans highway code i.e always overtake a cyclist, at great speed, close as possible, regardless of oncoming traffic. This is where I really started to take note of any available exit into roadside scrub/bushes/streams as a means of escaping death or serious injury.

While Clive pedalled towards Gruia many miles into the peasant country of south east Romania, Chris and I overtook him on the backroads, vaguely following the Danube. Here the twisting river had less consistent tow-pathing and, as time was pressing, the relatively traffic-friendly roads were a faster and better bet. As we bowled along in the old bus a man dressed smart-casually stepped out of an official looking car, parked at the side of the road and flagged us down. We wound our windows down and he peered in at Chris in the passenger seat. He had a knowing smirk on his face which gave us cause for concern.

"Engleeesh?" he questioned. "I am border police. What you doing in this part of Romania?"

Our answer to this, of course, made him smile as if his historic knowledge of Anglo Saxon eccentricity was confirmed. Then, "Passports, please." We furnished him with our beloved EU Identities. Then, "Oh. Chris, nice photo. Paul, your birthday next week. Happy birthday. Let me see in back of van please." By this stage we had relaxed. Our first impression of sneering implacability had been replaced by a feeling that we were dealing with a clever and ironic joker. He explained that border police tracked the areas a few miles in from the border crossings. "Drugs, migrants, criminals, men who hide from us," he explained.

He asked after our third member, "What his name?" We told him and said that he would likely be along shortly, panting away on two wheels. He smiled and, after warning us not to drink and drive, invited us to enjoy our evening and the delights of Romania. We breathed a sigh of relief as we motored on. Within a minute or two we realised that Clive had left his passport in the glove compartment. We debated returning to show our quirky border policeman Clive's credentials, but dismissed the idea as we weren't sure if Clive would take the same road and didn't want to risk giving up a passport. On we drove.

Inevitably, Clive cycled into the same border police.

10 miles short of Gruia I was cycling 3rd leg and on fairly quiet, straight road around Izvoarele in Romania. Probably because the road was just after one of the Serbian border bridges over The Danube, two policeman with car flagged me down. I was fairly relaxed initially (perhaps more so than I should have been). 'Hello Sir.' I was a little surprised that they seemed to know my nationality but also pleased that communication would be relatively easy. 'Passport please.' Ah, not so relaxed now as I knew I didn't have my passport.

'Sorry, I don't have it. I'm part of a cycle relay to Istanbul and my passport is in the support vehicle - a motorhome with my two friends.'

'Hmm...not good.' My heart sank especially as the communicating policeman seemed to be taking some pleasure in my discomfort. 'U really need to have ur passport with u at all times. It is a regulation.' There followed a long pause which I felt duty-bound to fill with a fawning apology.

'I really am sorry and I certainly will in future....Sir!' The fact that this seemed to amuse him still more was even more worrying.

'Yes... (long pause)...we have met ur friends in motorhome. They made no mention of ur passport... (long pause) but they did say they would have a cold beer ready for u in Gruia...have a good journey. Good day,' with an even broader smile. He obviously needed to get his kicks where he could on a lonely road near the Serbian border.

Chris and I wended our way to Gruia, a weaving quiet road. In the centre of the village we turned right down a steep track which hair-pinned its way towards the banks of the Danube. We arrived at a forlorn-looking encampment of scattered ramshackle buildings, a couple of rusted caravans, stray dogs and a large chalet style house that had seen much better days. A heavy bolted gate guarded the entrance to the place. We shouted. After a while a bosomy woman appeared, smiling, rouged, voluble. "Hi!" she yelled, "Welcome, I am Veron-ika. Only two, you say three on phone." We explained; she laughed opened the gates and the Mothership rumbled into the compound. Chris and I looked at each other and wondered what the hell we had booked into. At some point this large wooden lodge of a place might have seen better days but now it looked like a Romanian Mafioso hideaway where we could disappear without trace if the local cell decided it was for the best.

We told Veron-ika that we would wait for Clive. By now we knew of his encounter with the police. The sun was setting and we needed to relax and take stock. Clive wobbled down the escarpment to our hideaway, pleased to have the day done, unscathed. Meanwhile Veron-ika was mopping down our three-bed suite. Think outdoor pursuits shack-style dormitory. By the time she had finished the prevailing smell had metamorphosed from stale male sweat to pure Dettol. It was a moot point which was preferable.

Before showering we enquired about beer. Of course. There was a rickety terrace out back with a few tables scattered about waiting for Godot. Well, one table had a swarthy man slumped over a plastic two-litre bottle of crystal-clear firewater. He looked up as we sat down and our beers were delivered. We were wary. He wasn't. He had the odd word of English but seemed to rule the roost. He rasped something at Veron-ika and another giant bottle of the poteen appeared. Our man drunkenly insisted that we share the firewater experience with him. So shots had to be drunk in the early evening. Our benefactor, whose name sounded like a make of Vodka, caressed and then kissed Chris's bald head lovingly as some gesture of friendship. Clive and I laughed nervously. Chris claims he didn't enjoy it but we knew better.

Refreshed after showering we returned to the terrace for another weighty Balkan meal. By now our drunken buddy had a table full of swarthy and powerful looking men, mostly in combat fatigues, all looking forbidding. One of them, the youngest, say mid-twenties, was able to translate a little of our conversation. We gleaned a couple of things.

Firstly that there appeared to be dark dealings going on across the Danube; drugs, people trafficking, border patrols? We didn't feel threatened but we were pretty sure that these guys represented the darker side of Balkan life.

Secondly, they were enjoying Veron-ika's hospitality with the firm intention of getting wasted. I posted a video of our hostess on Facebook that night. It captures the boozy, subversive atmosphere of that remote terrace. Veron-ika is serving us and the deep animated growls of the men contrast with Chris's soft conversation as we enjoy our meal in the cool dark of that first evening in Romania, October 5th. The blurb that went with the footage ran like this:

.....stray dogs wandering about.. Men in combat fatigues. A degree of drunkenness. No threat, really apart from our host kissing Chris's head and touching him. Clive and I were embarrassed but we got a bit of touchy-feely ourselves. Odd drinking illegal booze on one side of the Danube while our hosts sneer at the Serbs across the water. In Gruia stray dogs and urchin children seem the norm. Life is peasant and hard. Again, though, the people are welcoming and open. We Brits are good at making others like us, it seems. Pleases and thank-yous go a long way.

I reflect now on this last comment. In several places we came across comments in praise of how British people conduct themselves. As I type this, on July 4th 2020 which has been dubbed Super Saturday as our lockdown is eased, I am not particularly enamoured of my countrymen and women. The hordes who invade beaches and gather at raves, the extremists who hijack the social and political agendas looking for fights, the drink-till-you-drop culture and reputation of Brits at home and abroad have all soured my view of my own people! In the hotels and shops and cafes and campsites we visited the prevailing opinion seemed to be that we Brits are good eggs. We aren't pushy or impolite. We apologise and thank; we smile and wait. I haven't tested this view on the Costa del Sol but certainly, in the Balkans, many other nationalities get a far worse press than we do. Starting with Americans and Japanese. Followed by anyone who isn't in the same tribe as whatever country we happened to be in.

And don't go anywhere near Black Lives Matter. We don't talk about such things, particularly in Bulgaria where England footballers were due to play a game made more tense by the apparent racism of the host fans. We would be in Sofia at the same time.

15
INTO BULGARIA AND THE BALKAN MOUNTAINS

The group stages of the Rugby World Cup were cranking up as we left The Danube and Romania behind. As we had traversed Europe cyclists had become an endangered species and now, turning away from the eastern route of the Danube as it snakes across to the Black Sea, we were to complete our journey on roads great and small, smooth and pitted, isolated and teeming. Chris set off early from Gruia the next morning. His first leg would take him across the border into Bulgaria at Calafat. Veron-ika sent us on our way with a breakfast of salami, cucumber, goat's cheese and omelette. Chunks of bread and black scented tea. Total damage for our stay, £15. Even cheaper than Mama Mila's hospitality!

On the tracks-called-roads out of Gruia the sights were grim. Stray dogs, fly-tipping and general rubbish littered the landscape. This south western corner of Romania is a poor and remote area that the EU coffers have yet to raise up. Dark, wizened women sit at roadsides, swaddled in dark shawls and headscarves, staring at passers-by out of deeply set eyes and with a wistful curiosity. Young men seem to work on the land or hang out in bars slurping the local hooch to while away the weekend hours. It's no wonder that the UK has seen large numbers of economic migrants, young hopefuls who come for work, for a better life.

As we headed to yet another border, this time into the north west of Bulgaria we hit the more important arterial roads. The EU economic machine became more obvious. Resurfacing of roads, more cars, more freight; fewer horses and carts; greater affluence.

Chris cycled through Pristo, Garla Mare, Salcia, Cetate, and Maglavit before getting to the impressive border crossing at Calafat. I was surprised that the road into Bulgaria was a motorway for the first couple of miles. I had no option but to get to the first turn off, release Clive for his stint, following the Danube on B roads through Dunavtsi, Achar and Dobri Dol to Lom. Chris, meanwhile, also had no option but to take the elevated motorway bridge back over the Danube out of Calafat before finding me at the first slip road, signpost Vidin. The headwinds on this high stretch of road meant that he had battled to cycle at walking pace. By the time he got to the Mothership, Clive was in the middle of a vast plain where flat land met the blue horizon as the Danube pressed on merrily a couple of miles to the north.

We were now in Montana territory which looked like what I imagined the vast open spaces of Montana USA to be like. Chris's stint had been long and arduous but Clive was on a flat stretch to Lom where I would take over for the last stage of the day into Montana town. Booking.com had suggested the Ogosta Hotel right in the centre earlier in the day. Mothership parking guaranteed. With the Danube behind us we now entered the Cyrillic confusion of Bulgarian road signs and our sketchy maps. We were off all cycle routes. As long as our phones were charged we would be OK, wouldn't we?

I took over and headed due south. The first five miles out of Lom were a nightmare. It was warm but the drizzle set in. For some reason the road to Rasovo was cobbled and vertiginous. I too was cycling at walking speed and panting like a dog in the desert. I remember fighting the compulsion to get off and walk. The boys hooted and waved as they passed me en-route to the hotel. Did I imagine laughter trailing back at me on the wind?

Once out of the hell that was Rasovo, I hit the open plain where flat land met the blue horizon. The weather perked up and, after a glitch or two, I found the boys parked up and booked in at the Ogosta. The hotel was hosting a wedding which was grand and epically eastern European. Bulgarian Eastern Orthodox Christian we were to learn. It was party central and we wondered if there would be any peace that night. Premiership footie was on the telly and swarthy, smiling, chunky men dressed up to the nines were crowding round the TV in reception, occasionally being shouted at by irate women. Children were running riot in the ballroom area. Some things don't change.

Chris had sussed out a restaurant via yet another dining app on his phone. We headed out of the hotel into an attractively pedestrianised town centre, then twisted this way and that in the dark before Chris found what he was looking for. It was a pizzeria. Quite a classy one, though. Chris was purring when we saw the menu and selection of wines and beers. He peaked too early in his praise of the joint when he said, "You can always tell a classy joint, linen napkins and warmed rolls to accompany the first course." While Chris and I were served with our starters, Clive's was forgotten. Then his main course was slow to arrive. Finally all his three courses arrived at the same time. Very classy indeed. Of course we didn't complain. We are British!

The Bulgarian wedding party was in its death throes when we got back but the debris littered the foyer when we headed out for coffee in the main square the following morning. Clive had picked a route to take us to the capital, Sofia, avoiding the main arterial route but cutting through the Balkan mountains to avoid the worst excesses of gradient. We were in uncharted territory and on busy roads with lumbering juggernauts and, worse, boy racers who sped past bicycles within inches. No quarter given. Drivers were unused to seeing men on bikes and, while lorry drivers seemed to slow and take wide berths past us, saloon speed merchants didn't give a monkey's.

Chris cycled out of Montana and a more hilly ride as he headed south. The Balkan mountains rose majestically on either side and our route had to take in some serious gradients on a busy road. We had each seen lone women standing at roadsides and, we assumed, waiting for buses. As Chris cycled on he realised that curb-side prostitution was alive and kicking in north Bulgaria. He stopped for a breather near the top of a steep climb and engaged a lone female in a conversation redolent of innuendo. Romanian he guessed as her accent sounded a little French. Her English bettered his Romanian.

"You're nearly there," she purred, as Chris caught his breath and smiled.

"I've got a few miles to go. Is the road difficult further on?" Chris responded, rather weakly.

"Depends what you mean by difficult. I've always found it quite easy," came the cryptic and cheeky reply. Chris had no idea how to handle the conversation, so before he got invited behind the bus shelter for a full explanation, he took a swig of his energy drink and pedalled on, furiously.

I took over on the flatter run by-passing Vatsra before handing over to Clive for the more tricky, busy main road into Sofia. As the traffic intensified near the ring road, we took to the Mothership for safety's sake. Clive had experienced a couple of heart-stopping moments in dark tunnels and discretion became the better part of valour. We had booked a hotel on the Southern edge of Sofia. Having done the touristy thing a year earlier on our fact finding mission, we wanted only to crack on. It was 7th October. We were due in Istanbul on the 12th. Clive and Chris remembered the hundred miles or so into Sophia like this.

Clive. Day 23: Montana to Sofia. OK to start with but became a bit of a nightmare with 70 mph tunnels which, I, having walked one via the narrow walkway, became traumatised at the thought of doing so again. Mothership pick-up for last few miles into city. Stayed at hotel which, rather like Visegrad's, flattered to deceive with a rather 'fur coat, no knickers' atmosphere.

Chris. Brilliant Clive. My encounter with heavily made up "lady" in lay by at the top of a long, lorry-filled hill. I stopped to ask if I was near the top yet. She said something in French to the effect that a happy ending could be in sight! Ah, I thought, the cogs in my mind slowly working. Poor girl, waiting for punters to take into the bushes for a quickie. I was too tired anyway! But, lots of these girls on the Bulgarian roads - sad way to have to make a living.

I posted the following blog that evening.

Late afternoon and we have arrived in Sofia after some testing gradients over the Balkan mountains. The E79 sliced through a few monsters which might have found the old men dismounting - but we all stayed in the saddle. As we neared Sofia the teeming traffic, the loss of hard shoulder and the pitch black long tunnels, reduced speed to a crawl. Clive hit a dangerous situation so the Mothership swept him up and prescribed strong coffee.

The abiding memories of today will be the magnificence of the mountains, the overpowering stench of diesel, the never ending piles of rubbish blighting the roadsides and villages...and some interesting roadside individuals selling their services...

...Clive's snoring means that he has to sleep as far away as possible from Chris. Paul has to play piggy in the middle. We are slumped with beers in hand...Plovdiv tomorrow. We're dreaming of a Turkish bath and massage on arrival in Istanbul. Our ladies will be there to massage...our egos.

Clive's 'fur coat, no knickers' description was of our hotel which seemed to be built to impress Russian oligarchs but since Bulgaria's entry into the EU they had lost some of the Russian mafia money. Pure speculation of course, but the bling of chandeliers, floor to ceiling heavy curtains, garish flocked wallpaper and ugly gargoyle fountains hardly matched the current workaday clientele which we encountered. It had been a difficult day and we were pleased to have arrived safely. We had the length of Bulgaria to travel in the next couple of days and no safe river paths, only main roads and the whistle of overtaking traffic.

Some experienced saddle-men might question our 'route A to goal' approach. From Sofia we planned to take route 8 (an A road) which Clive and I knew well, to slice south east through Bulgaria to the Kapikule border with Turkey. We could have navigated a meandering ride for a quieter, perhaps safer journey in a due-southerly direction into Greece before cutting back east into Turkey. However, time and speed and our pre-planning had each played their part in suggesting that the more direct, as-the-crow-flies route would be OK and get us to the Blue Mosque in Istanbul in just under the month. So, for good or ill, we stuck to the plan. The weather was with us, we just hoped that the roads would not prove to be the death of us.

16
DRAWING BREATH IN PLOVDIV

After a difficult day getting to Sofia, the road to Plovdiv was busy but, for the most part, flat. Potholes helped to slow the hot-rod maniacs and our confidence grew as the teeming traffic of Sofia gave way to calmer cycling conditions. We left our overnight hostelry, the Montecito, a cross between a Russian oligarch's dacha and a faux Italian renaissance museum. The morning fog was a pall of smog over the capital. I didn't fancy the first leg much but bit the bullet. My luck was in. The sun fought its way through to help me with the steep climb out of Sofia.

Out of the city on Route 8 it is rough country. Still plenty of dogs on chains to guard dilapidated homesteads. Peasant greengrocers line the highway every few hundred metres. On colourful display are enormous distended squashes, 3ft high leek-like triffids and giant watermelons. More *Beware Wild Boar* signs add to the roadside fun along with cartoon cut-out police cars which, from a distance look like the real thing. A much more pleasant way to calm traffic!

However, maniac drivers seem unconcerned by speed limits. Police hide in the cities and let the Lewis Hamiltons enjoy themselves double-overtaking on the country roads. Brilliant and breathtaking but ...bloody hell! Route 8 is Roman-straight with shrines at black spots from Novi Khan to Kostanets to Septemvri. Indeed all the way to Plovdiv. We frightened boys kept tight to the kerb, if there was one. Mostly the macho men floored their accelerators and left us alone. I shouldn't overstate the danger. We might have been nervous at times but vision was good and we didn't wobble too much.

We hadn't booked a hotel in Plovdiv and Bulgarians don't go in for camping in October. Scrolling through Booking.com (again) we found two Park Hotels, one at 1200 Lev (£600) for two nights and the other at 200 Lev. We made a predictable error and Clive had to talk our way out of posh Park and into affordable Park. So much the better actually since affordable Park, less than a mile from the town centre, had Mothership parking and a bicycle park outside the front. We had a room with a view - of the go-kart track and football stadium. Perfect.

We met Mikhael, barman, on arrival who presented us with a complimentary tonic with ice and lemon. For 3 Lev (£1.50) he asked if we would like gin added. No brainer. No brainer for a second either. We sat in the foyer and agreed that we were as much mentally tired as anything. A day tomorrow looking round the old town of Plovdiv would be a real treat - and the first day for a while that we hadn't crawled out of bed as dawn broke. Chris was already playing with Google to find a classy eatery to service his refined palate.

Plovdiv was the 2019 European City of Culture. The redeveloping of the city centre, which Clive and I had noted the previous year, had galloped on apace. So much so, in fact, that we struggled to recall the geography of the place. The cobbled old town is a charming tourist trap and Chris duly bought a Russian/Bulgarian doll for his granddaughter as we wandered about in the sunshine of the following day. The centre of town is a pedestrianised delight. The amphitheatre has been excavated and made pristine. Cafes and bars throng with young Bulgarians. The physiognomy of the Balkan races can be confusing. Swarthy, dark, square-jawed and squat one minute; olive-skinned or sallow and auburn the next. What you rarely see is black people. When a beautiful black girl sat on the amphitheatre steps near us, we commented on the surprise. Strange. In the context of the brewing controversy over racism in football, the Bulgarians had become infamous for overt racism on the terraces. With England due to play the following week, the F.A. had asked for guarantees of safety and freedom from abuse. The President of the Bulgarian football union, Borislav Mihaylov, replied by, basically, saying *get your own house in order*. This didn't go down well with either UEFA or, indeed Borislav's own Prime Minister. He was instructed to resign. The game itself was halted twice after England players suffered monkey chants and Nazi salutes. So the Bulgarian team manager, Krasimir Balakov, was the next to fall on his sword.

I asked our genial barman Mikhael about all this. He was guarded in his response, his eyes darting over my shoulder to see who might be listening. He said that his people weren't racist, that they were as likely to be unpleasant to other 'tribes' as he called them as to those of different skin colour. He alluded to his own discriminatory experiences given his, implied, sexual orientation. He was a highly articulate guy who had spent some time working in London and made reference to how easy it was to make judgements from the vantage point of a multicultural world city. Other people's lives and experiences differed. I understood what he was saying, I guess, but didn't quite buy the excuse.

Back home and a little ironically Extinction Rebellion were marching in London and Boris's timetable for a Brexit deal seemed doomed. Well here I am typing in July 2020 and not much has changed on that front, virus or no virus.

The other item amongst many which caught my eye was the apparently imminent Turkish invasion of the area of Kurdish-held territory on its southern border with Syria. As we were about to enter Turkey, albeit many miles from the Syrian border, we were to hear the probable truth that Turkey has helped out many thousands more Syrian refugees (by giving them bed, food and hospital facilities in migrant camps in a border buffer zone) than the rest of Europe put together. Interesting it was to be in places where the 'take' on global stories is so very different from that of our liberal media and our 'we know best' tendency in foreign policy. I won't blather on about it because what do I know?

Meanwhile, back on the streets of Plovdiv, Chris and I found a wine store which gave us a few tasting glasses of Rosé.

We promised to return actually to buy something (we did!) but Chris was on a mission to seek out a craft beer bar which his app had singled out as THE place to go. Clive was more concerned with strolling about so Chris dragged me to the Cat and Mouse, on Hristo Dyukmedzhiev in the Kapana district, a five minute walk away. Simply the best bar in town! What Andre our host didn't know about beer wasn't worth knowing. We texted Clive immediately, *get over here*. Andre boasted 150 beers from all over the world. A Dowdeswell heaven. I took plenty of photos within and without. Plovdiv is a fine and cheap city break and an enchanting place. Mostly unknown to Brits, it is Bulgaria's second city with a population of nearly 400,000. We cyclists tapped into a fraction of what it had to offer. I would return in a heartbeat.

The next morning, Day 26, 10th October, Clive discovered that his bill at reception for a service wash of his smalls amounted to about £40. I had told him that fresh undies were an expensive luxury but he just wouldn't listen.

We headed out of town and found Route 8 again. Chris pedalled away but quickly alerted us to problems. The low autumnal sun was blinding, even with sunglasses and this, combined with wind and teeming traffic led us all to agree: too dangerous. We sat and mused in the Mothership but Clive had set the decision-making standards. Basically all for one and one for all. Chris recalls his hesitancy as a 'wimpy act'. He went on:

...sun in my eyes, won't be able to see etc, etc - it was bloody dangerous but as usual Clive volunteered to "test it out". Good man. Hard yakka on the road to Edirne that day.

After a calming coffee Clive ventured forth. The sun was higher and we made good progress to the border. The last mile or two had to be negotiated on the motorway. While bicycles are allowed, amazingly, on the hard shoulder, we decided that the Mothership could take us the short hop from Route 8 to the border crossing close by. We remembered the long freight queues going both ways at the border and they seemed even longer as we scuttled past.

Memories of Clive's and my last dealings at the Kapikule customs were clear in our minds. I scanned the various border personnel for familiar faces. No such luck. The Mothership, a considerable curiosity was inspected and passed the dog sniffer tests with flying colours. We were just thinking that our smooth passage was too good to be true when we were directed to a payment kiosk just beyond the Turkish customs check.

17
EDIRNE AND SILIVRI: ALMOST THERE

Clive had the paperwork for taking the Mothership into Turkey and knew that an insurance charge would be levied at the border. What we weren't prepared for was that they wouldn't take credit or debit cards. I recorded our frustrations:

> *Border shenanigans. Ninety minutes to get our papers vetted by a series of quite smiley Bulgars and Turks. 175 euros to insure the Mothership, cash only, paid at D3 one of several customs stations for the fleecing of innocent European Unionists. 'Dollar, Turkish Lira or Euro. No pounds sterling, thank you,' said our smiling cashier. The stock of our currency has slumped, it seems.*

We felt sure that we had seen others ahead of us in the payment queue, handing over Visa cards or similar. As we scraped together a combination of Euros and Lira, we wondered if our genial cashier was going to trouser our cash. No matter. We were in!

I took to the bike for the twenty miles or so into Edirne. I well remembered the route through the town centre past the great Selimiye Mosque to the little backstreet where the Mothership was parked outside the well-remembered Selimiye Hotel. Weirdly in this hotbed of Islam, Ave Maria was playing on a loop in the lift. Odd.

Clive and I retraced our steps of the year before and took Chris into town, through the vibrant bazaar where sweets are piled high at every other stall with clothes and shoes and cakes filling the gaps. The pedestrianised centre hums along and the call to prayer from the speakers on the minarets was rather obviously ignored. We made it back to Jon's Bar at the end of town and delighted in the Turkish EFES ale. As we wandered across the road to eat, I pointed out to Clive his route out of town for the following day. Did he take any notice? Not a chance.

We observed the cultural shift from southern Bulgaria. Northern Turkey seemed immediately more affluent. In this part of Turkey money is being pumped into infrastructure projects, mosques and business and residential premises. Erdogan's agenda seems clear - build, build, build and pursue an increased emphasis on religious conservatism. Once again we enjoyed our time in Edirne but we were now so close that we were savouring the end being in sight. One last push.

Clive got lost, predictably, on his way out of Edirne the following morning. The D100 would take us all the way to Istanbul. Just over a hundred miles we calculated. Much of the road we had driven earlier in the year but the traffic heading for the capital seemed more intense than we remembered. We were surprised by wind and rain but we had been spoilt for much of the trip so we felt it to be our just desserts. The road alternated between single and dual carriageway. Thankfully a new motorway had been built to ease some of the speeding thunder. The hard shoulders were wide and we managed pretty well but Chris complained about a tiring headwind, while I luxuriated in the social media love of it being my birthday! 68 for me and 82 for the great man, Sir Bobby Charlton.

I can't say that the main road cycling in northern Turkey was a bundle of laughs but we managed with just a few hairy moments. We saw no other cyclists as we each ploughed our steady furrows keeping tight to kerbsides and concentrating hard. We interchanged riders rather more because of the wearying nature of concentration and the long slow uphill climbs. As Chris and I waited at a rendezvous we were engaged in conversation by a couple of engineers who were parked, like us, at the roadside, having a snack. We told them what we were doing - cue astonished but admiring smiles - then they revealed that they were engineers and part of a team planning and building a high speed rail link from Istanbul to Sofia. Planning problems? No, we have a lot of spare land. What if people complain? A smile and a shrug. How long from start of the project to the end? A year, maybe a little more. Thoughts of the spiralling costs of HS2, never mind the feasibility of the project in the first place.

We made the 100+ miles to Silivri in fair time but couldn't locate the campsite we had earmarked for the night. We did find one windswept ghost town of a place with static caravans which seemed shut up for the season. We bumped into yet another kindly woman who tried to get in touch with the site owners for us. After an incomprehensible three way exchange via phone, woman and Chris, we abandoned all hope and set off to find a bed before the night swallowed us up.

As luck would have it we happened on a roadside hotel which looked rather out of our league until Chris, with his smooth negotiating skills seemed to seal a remarkable deal. Rather like the silly antiques programmes where a celebrity antiques person offers a fraction of the asking price for a priceless bit of silver and the vendor says, *Yes, alright I'll give you a 95% discount*, so too the manager on reception at the Kumburgaz Marin Princess Hotel. Chris wangled a three bedroomed suite on the tenth floor for a song. The boys gave me cake and ale for my birthday in the room and there is a sparkling video to record it. I chatted to my nearest and dearest and felt pretty festive. We were just sixty miles from Istanbul.

The bar was welcoming and a cool piano was being tinkled nearby. A few yards from the hotel we found a very average restaurant but it did the job. Local Raki provide by our host helped to dull the senses and make the pain of the bill bearable. I say pain but since we had left Austria pretty much all our bills had been half the price what anything would come to in England. Our girls would be flying in to see us the following morning. Surely the last day's cycling wouldn't be too arduous? We would be skirting the beaches of the Sea of Marmara, the inland body of water which connects the Black and the Aegean Seas and runs into Istanbul and the Bosphorus. Exotic stuff!

Chris took a video of me cycling off the next morning after breakfasting in a vast ballroom of a sea-viewing dining hall. I hit traffic and difficult, not to say dangerous, road conditions almost as soon as I had set off. There was no escape from the main D100 dual carriageway and as I neared the great city the arterial routes criss-crossing the main drag complicated matters. I was glad to meet Chris at the beach about thirty miles out of Istanbul. We had tea and sat on the beach and paddled in the Marmara, while Clive pedalled on. Chris was to do the glory leg into the city but the entry into Sultanahmet on the western shore of the Bosphorus was more laboured than triumphal due to the dead ends of road and building works which slowed his progress. He finally found the blue cycle path - the first we had seen in several hundred miles - and entered the old city to group hugs and whoops of relief and joy. Clive and I had checked in to our old friend the Hotel Acra and, amazingly, found an Ottopark with a space for a weary Mothership. Chris weaved his way along the sea front and into the twisting cobbled street of Sultanahmet . The tight streets of this tourist quarter were teeming with people and coaches and cars but when he arrived we finally knew that we were safe and sound and jubilant. We had done it!

PART III
AFTER

1
CAROUSING IN ISTANBUL

When Chris cycled up the cobbled Caddesi Amiral Tafdil at around 2pm on the 12th October, the three old men walked his Halford's Boardman special around to the Otto-parked Mothership. I had backed the old girl through the eye of a needle, guided by an Ottopark expert, well-versed in stacking as many vehicles as possible into the already crammed piece of rough ground. The van's rest was to be short-lived but for now she had a stunning view of the city and the Bosphorus. We had become oblivious to the heavy stench inside the van and our bikes were caked in mud and the scrapes and scratches of the last month. The afternoon sun was beating down. Fumigation could wait. The boys went for a celebratory beer on the Akbiyik Caddesi, vibrant with bars and restaurants. Clive and I knew it well. Incongruously this westernised fun-street nestles round the corner from the Blue Mosque and Hagia Sophia, the emblems of devout Islam and ancient Ottoman culture.

The girls had alerted us of their arrival at Istanbul Airport. Since January a new and palatial air hub had been opened to the north of the city. The Ataturk Airport, previously host to international arrivals had been closed. Too small? Ataturk's reputation as the moderniser of Turkey and his political pushing of the country towards westernisation has fallen foul of Erdogan's desire to re-establish his own version of religious and political fundamentalism. Anyway Ataturk Airport is closed and the new one is much further from the city centre. The ladies had had a less fraught journey into the city than the men but we had a joyful reunion as their taxi pulled up outside the Acra Hotel. Shower or G and T? Sarah Dowdeswell didn't draw breath before her answer.

We re-engaged with our old friend with Huddersfield connections. Endre had moved to the restaurant next door but all the colourful outlets along this buzzy tourist strip dish out the same, sexy Turkish fare. And EFES beer. Karen of course with her regime of immunosuppressant drugs and gluten-free food has to be constantly alert to the potential problems of what she puts into her body. This has no effect on her effervescent nature and, as the queen of the photo-iPad, her shots of central Europe and, now Istanbul are remarkable. She brought with her the thanks and updates from the BeatSCAD team.

Remarkably the total had soared past £5000 - and this from a fairly modest reach-out from the three families.

The weather was set fair for the next few days. Karen and Clive had planned to cram in as much sightseeing as possible in the next 36 hours before taking themselves and the Mothership back home. The following day, October 13th, was Belinda's birthday and celebrations were in order! We breakfasted in the extraordinary basement dining area once more - amid the ruins of King Constantine's Palace. Check out the Acra Hotel's website for information on this and the extraordinary history of ancient Constantinople. Istanbul is a vast melting pot of the old and new. Giant building projects dot the skyline in a Manhattan facsimile, while the old cobbled streets and shabby chic of central Istanbul maintain its evocative eastern feel.

We had planned a triumphant photo opportunity at the blue Mosque but mistakenly had our mugshots taken outside the Hagia Sophia, so much for our architectural knowledge! Karen and Belinda had brought the wherewithal for a We've Done It! banner and so Facebook was splattered with the three old men in fluorescent, lime green, BeatSCAD cycling gear with bike and banner in front of the great museum. I wrote:

Tuesday October 13th. Belinda's birthday. Day 1 of no biking. Photo shoot in front of the Hagia Sophia. This caused a bit of a stir. Tourists thought we were celebs. We didn't disabuse them. The Japanese took photos, of course. Then we ferried across the Bosphorus so Clive could say that he got on a bike in Asia. The Mothership needed some TLC to prepare it for the journey back (de-fumigation). Clive and Karen have stepped up big time to nurture the motor we have called 'home' back to Blighty.

The Spice Market was a must as was a rooftop beer, just spitting distance from the iconic temples of this teeming city. We have celebrated B's birthday well...so far. This city pulsates with life. High rise blocks dominate skylines near and far and yet the vast mosques of old trump the new. The Bosphorus is a busy waterway shuttling workers and tourists east to west and vice versa. Romans, Byzantines and Ottomans built and prospered in Constantinople.

Constantine made himself emperor in 300 and something AD and was the first Christian Roman emperor. Greeks, Persians *and Alexander the Great had all enjoyed power in this place but the Ottoman/Turk won the longer game. Constantinople became Istanbul in 1923. Enough of history, let's live for the moment.*

We had lunch in Asia and were reminded of the social and religious conservatism of most of Turkey. Here the welcome was warm and indulgent but no alcohol was served in the restaurants. We asked our friendly host in his hilltop bistro for an explanation and he indicated that away from the centre of the city the local mosques exert their influence over the community atmosphere and liberties. He wasn't complaining, merely pointing out that much of Turkey operates under different rules from those areas of high tourist intensity. As we ate in his cafe, gigantic container ships eased their way through the Bosphorus to the Black sea. I took multiple photos of these. Containers the size of houses piled high atop each other on a long boat the size of a football pitch. What a vital trade hub this is.

We returned for Belinda's birthday rooftop drinks. The girls had bought her a ceramic plate and bowls to which she had taken a shine. We raised our glasses while looking across the roofs and waters of this exotic city. Then on to the weirdly named Honest John's restaurant, also on the Abiyik Caddesi. The following day Clive and Karen would set off hoping to have a bit of a touring holiday as they - and the Mothership - retraced the wheel revolutions of three old men.

We waved them off the next morning with our bikes and some fetid washing as cargo to remind them of us. They intended to take a lazy ten days. Their ferry back across the Channel, booked for Friday 25th October, would give Karen just enough time to dash to a SCAD conference in Newcastle and Clive to drive directly to the Scorpions Hockey Club Biennial lunch at Hampton Wick where money and mickey taking had been pledged. Madness. Chris and I would meet him there and don our lycra and SCAD tops one more time for an embarrassing cycle-lap of honour in Bushey Park. The things we do for charity.

Belinda and I had booked a couple of nights in another part of Sultanahmet at the curiously named Hotel Sphendon. Chris and Sarah opted for a waterfront Radisson. Pampering for the stylish couple was needed. The building works diminished the grandeur of the setting but Belinda and I much enjoyed rooftop drinks with them before a meal on the Galata Bridge which bestrides the Golden Horn and has a special place in the history and romance of Istanbul. Its exotic past wasn't matched by the pleasant but overpriced meal. Location, location, location. What a memorable time it was, spending a few hours relaxing with great friends after such an adventure. The chance to savour the moment for a few short days was special. My final post reads:

Of Mosques and Men

As my stomach loses its washboard tautness and thighs reduce from Hoy-like girth to stringy saplings, home thoughts from abroad are infiltrating.

What an extraordinary city this is. East meet West; Europe and Asia, cultures clash and the old fights with the new. Istanbul is massive and despite the high rise panorama across the Bosphorus, the mosques, markets, temples and tombs, spices and scents tussle hard with the incipient modernity. They haven't lost the war just yet.

And talking of war...the military activity on the Syrian border is all over the news channels here. Naturally the Euro soccer match versus France last night took precedence for the evening. As we wandered the streets of Sultanahmet we were, as usual, assailed by a hundred men imploring us to try their shish or kofte. Bright appetite-suppressant photos fill the vast menus on display along each jostling boulevard. The men are polite, funny, insistent, urgent even. They want your custom; their lives depend on it. As you pass there is no rancour. Have a nice day.

Chris and I pulled on skirts to enter the Blue Mosque. The Hagia Sophia demanded less of us. The tombs and churches of Sultanahmet and Fatih demand revisiting. This is a place where many faiths have ebbed and flowed. Now the Turkish leader is ensuring that monuments of Islam are as much a building priority as high rise office blocks. The huge Camlica Mosque, the largest in Turkey, was opened in March of this year in Uskudar on the Anatolian (eastern) shore of the Bosphorus. We ticked the boxes of the amazing Grand Bazaar and Suleymaniye Mosque complex. We wandered through slum areas which sat incongruously adjacent to high-rise developments. The exotic buzz of ancient and modern was captivating in the autumn sunshine.

One could dwell on the Galata Bridge looking across to Asia as the dozens of fisherman land their quivering catches to sell to the restaurants which lurk on the tier below. We ate at one such and saw the teeming boat traffic of tourists and traders shuttle about. An exotic, chaotic facsimile of Sydney Harbour. Intoxicating.

And now we're going home. We said farewells to Chris and Sarah. Clive and Karen are speeding up through Bulgaria and the poor old Mothership has incurred more fines for trundling along without motorway permits - amongst other things. The old lady has not deserved such ill treatment at home and abroad. Clive has already written to Sadiq Khan about London and its attachment to Big Brother. He'll need to repeat the dose in several languages before the Mothership rolls into Harwich on the 25th October.

And so we say farewell.
Enough, no more.
See y'all back in Blighty.
BeatSCAD.

2
DOWN TO EARTH WITH A THUMP:
A BALL OF CONFUSION

What has followed our return from Istanbul has been further political upheaval followed by apocalyptic nightmare. My views on Boris and Brexit do not need to be aired again, here. I'm writing this bit on the 10th June and we are coming up to three months of lockdown with death tolls beginning to subside but, perhaps, not as quickly as jobs and the economy evaporate before our eyes. The murder of George Floyd in Minnesota has ignited something else altogether. The world, from where we sit on our capitalist first world perches, seems such a different place. As statues are being torn down and Black Lives Matter has grabbed the world agenda, let's hope this isn't yet another false dawn for the underprivileged and marginalised. The media, so quick to jump on bandwagons, so quick to present a liberal 'woke' spin, need to play their part in contextualising. Their emphasis in lockdown has been to dramatise and criticise; blame more than scrutinise, pessimism far more than optimism. Perhaps they have had just cause. In dealing with the Saddam-like pulling down of the Edward Colston statue in Bristol, it was our somewhat maligned Police who showed restraint and judgement. We could all learn a little from this. Interesting that, despite a flurry of left v right standoffs, the public monument debate has moved on properly. The activists are talking.

One of the threats which could become an opportunity is the inability of UK citizens to head off for summer holidays abroad. Staycation has become a reality for most of us. The simplicity of a tent, a bike, a garden space, a paddling pool, a barbecue; time with kids, with family, hailing strangers on a walk; taking time over breakfast; cobwebs on the car, working from home, discovering zoom. The Thursday applause for the NHS and the community spirit generated, along with Rishi Sunak's handouts, have done just a little to offset the family tragedies which will continue into the future, either directly or indirectly because of Covid 19.

Our bike trip would be impossible now, of course but it was, in essence, very simple and inexpensive. And yet we derived so much more from it than from a poolside holiday in Ibiza. And now simplicity and creativity in our leisure seems to be imperative!

Jump forward a month.

It's now 6th July and observations made only a short while ago seem obsolete. We have just had Super Saturday, the crazy day of lockdown easing. Premiership footballers all take the knee. Estate agents are worrying about calling the main bedroom of a house the Master because they imagine it has potential for offence owing to its possible association with colonial enslavement. Ye Gods. Perhaps that expletive is offensive? Clapping for the NHS is over but holiday bridges are the coming thing. We Brits are clearly seen as people who want to get rousingly pissed on a regular basis and swelter in the sun on the Costa del Sol.

I'll try to make a few salient updates before this goes to press but that great song by The Temptations, 'Ball of Confusion', slid into my mind. In 1970 I danced to it. In 2020 I listened to it. Do check it out. It's an extraordinary protest/state of the world song. There is a huge amount of confusion around. Debate has been stymied by a fundamental unwillingness of those with an opinion to listen to anyone else's view. Left or right. Town and country. Black and White.

And so it goes on. Trump doesn't help but nor do many others, including ourselves. The lack of nuance and perspective has been lost in our so-called civilised society. Trust in our leaders, in each other seems to have been shot away. We are all reeling in the wake of the Covid pandemic.

People like we three old men and their ladies have, to some extent, lived our lives and paid our dues. I don't fear for us but our ageing and moderate and experienced voices can no longer be heard over the woke pandemonium of the virtue-signalling obsessives.

I fear for those younger than us who have the precarious world of jobs and child rearing and trying to eke out some fulfilment in the years ahead; of making sense of new realities; of trying to build a life in a society where the freedoms that my generation enjoyed have been hijacked by an unnuanced, self-righteous agenda - both on the left and right of politics. I fear for the manipulation of facts; of truth. I worry that the majority whisper politely while the few shout them down. There is, of course, cause for optimism in the causes taken up by so many young people. In particular human rights, the environment and the greater clarity with which they see the charlatans in our political firmament.

Where are the leaders? Where are the politicians who can look beyond the expediency of vote-catching?

3
ABROAD THOUGHTS FROM HOME

When we had all arrived back in dear old Blighty, on October 16th, we were aware that there was a short window of interest in our exploits. Nothing worse than a biking bore and each of us resolved to recount tales when asked but keep a lid on the grandstanding. The business of getting on with life and, in Clive's case, dreaming up another silly challenge, took over. No time to rest on laurels.

Chatting with the lads now there still remains the glow of doing something impressive. I asked them to reflect back on the experience and what the great positives were. Not just the obvious delights much recorded here of people, places and the satisfaction of a physical challenge completed but the more subtle and smaller pleasures which might not have been predicted.

The destructive atmosphere of Brexit and all the political and social baggage which had dogged our conversations for nearly four years seemed to lighten as we moved east. Our phones could tell us what was trending on Twitter or what drama the BBC's Laura Kuenssberg was working up at Westminster but we were increasingly content at being out of touch. Here we were in the heart of Europe and welcomed at campsites, in bars, in cities and off the beaten track. The Brexit chatter in Holland, Germany and Austria gave way to unconcern and disinterest as we moved from obviously first world economies to those nations trying to catch up with the European ideal. To get to Turkey and Asia we had pedalled through The Netherlands, Germany, Austria, Slovakia, Hungary, Croatia, Serbia, Romania and Bulgaria. After Austria we would see a different, remote and more impoverished Europe but our welcomes were, almost without exception, warm. I can't overstate how calming it is to be free of the dispiriting effects of media. The Westminster bubble and the divisions that our politicians have created are heavy weights to carry around. The three of us felt much the lighter for being removed from England.

That is not to say that we weren't aware of the recent and historic turmoil of the Balkans. It doesn't take much research to establish the view that the tribes dislike each other. The reconfiguration of the Balkans, the changing of names, does not eradicate the recent tragedies of Kosovo and Bosnia. There are plenty of refugees from this savage period of ethnic cleansing living in the UK. They have frightful tales to tell. The three old men didn't discuss with, say, our Serbian hosts, the massacre of 8000 male Bosnians at Srebrenica. Knowing of the recent and bloody internecine savagery, the febrile atmosphere on our home front in July 2020, pales somewhat.

Freed from the imprisonment of media we were enjoying each other's company with conversation ranging over so many things both intimate and bantering. Spurs came in for some heavy damage when Bayern Munich put them to the sword 7-2 on October 1st. Chris went into a personal meltdown in the Mothership. No sympathy from Clive and me. Even Spurs's wayward fortunes seemed a little less important in our biking bubble. Chris at least was pleased that our use of phones had been cut to checking Google maps and locating campsites. No way was he going to tune in to the 5 Live commentary after the second goal went in. The Rugby World Cup would come to its climax after our return and the early group fixtures almost passed us by.

Our phones became practical tools, not obsessive, nail-biting social imperatives. Google maps, iSharing and booking.com were our go-to sites. Most evenings Chris would get his digits to search for local bars or restaurants. We found that even in remote Serbian wastelands Mr Google could find us a beer and a bed for the night. Increasingly we needed the connectivity as campsites started to close and our creaking bodies fancied proper beds and proper showers. Early on we had recognised that a certain level of fitness and freedom from injury were essential but a decent set of toilets and shower facilities came a close second. The added advantage of phone technology helps enormously. Reverse reading Rhine maps proved weirdly successful but the confidence that Google maps and GPS tracking can give is considerable. This didn't prevent each of us getting lost on several occasions, the most embarrassing being the time it took Clive and I to find the Mothership, which we had parked in a suburban side street on the outskirts of Vienna a couple of days earlier. We headed through the Prater Park, along the Hauptalle which borders the great park, cycling in exactly the wrong direction.

Our phones also gave us some problems. We had each paid extra for what we thought would be packages freed of roaming charges. As we had slipped from one country to the next we were welcomed, of course, by a new national network. As the UK was still in the EU we naively imagined that our roaming would be free; not so. Our 'bundles' required boosting to the tune of a few hundred pounds between us. Not disastrous but annoying. My provider, the excellent Utility Warehouse (plug!) who, I think, use EE, were helpful (turn off your data when you can, allow us to increase your top up limit and don't use your phone in Turkey unless you're on a hotel wifi) but each of us registered a degree of pissed-offedness.

Moreover each of our phones picked up different networks. I don't know for how long Clive's phone thought he was in Serbia as we trundled through Romania and into Bulgaria, but it was a good 48 hours. Of course the Serbs look across the Danube and scowl at the Bulgars and vice versa. The phone signals mix across the water far more harmoniously. We all commented on how the simple life works. An active day, harmonious interactions and simple pleasures make for happy chaps.

The fitness thing is interesting. We were each pretty bike-fit by the time we wobbled into Istanbul. The incentive of the project had given us the edge to get into shape. It would have been idiocy not to. Since our return we have each been more idle. Clive and Chris have managed a few gentle excursions on two wheels. My weighty Carrera has sat gathering garage cobwebs. Joe Wicks has not enticed me into early morning physical jerks. I know that I will return to a fitness regime. It's in the blood. The Eye2i gave us a purpose. Exercise without purpose = Boredom. Zoom fitness doesn't do it for me.

We had been reasonably fit before setting off and had been rather blasé about our medical histories. Clive had a heart attack in 2012 which gave rise to a couple of stents being implanted. His narrowboat nickname became *Two Stents.* We each took cocktails of drugs which seem to be the dietary supplements for men of our age. Prevention rather than cure. We classed our little adventure as a cycling holiday and so didn't bother to check our travel insurances too carefully. Of course we were still in the European Union at time of travel and so our E111 medical cards were still active. Not for long, I guess.

Spending too much time pondering the what ifs before setting out on challenges can be a recipe for inertia. Poor health, continual bad weather, bike problems, Mothership problems and accidents were all risks to be assessed...and put in their place. On returning we could only thank our lucky stars that all had gone so well. The problems we had, of getting lost, of Chris's crash, of wild dogs and teeming traffic and dark tunnels, of border crossings and paperwork, were dealt with at the time - and we moved on. The major hangover has been the Mothership's traffic violations. Might as well blame an inanimate machine for the crimes of her masters.

Recently I asked my buddies what worries about home they had harboured while cycling. Chris's first thoughts were for Sarah and the wider Dowdeswell clan. Would his grandchildren, Rex and Lola, recognise him? Sarah had to manage the ongoing house works: rendering, paving, cladding. Chris's attempts at micromanaging from the Balkans weren't entirely successful. No surprise there. Chris's business was in a certain limbo. Monitoring emails is one thing but when clients know that you are on a bicycle a couple of thousand miles away, credibility is stretched.

I had fewer worries on my plate although Covid 19 has given me the missing-grandchildren syndrome this year. I was in regular contact with Belinda and my children, Laura and Charlie, the latter enjoying his own escapades in Japan at the Rugby World Cup. I'm quite a phlegmatic guy, at least that's the impression I seem to give others. The narrow focus of our Eye2i project suited me. I had felt both excited and calm as each cycling day dawned.

As for Clive, well he admits that in years gone by he would have been very worried about leaving Karen, given her parlous state of health. However, since the hiatuses of liver transplant and heart attacks, she has been remarkably fit and healthy. Her gold medals at successive transplant games bear witness to her condition! Clive pointed out that in our digital world, he was able to see and hear Karen each day and catch up on each other's news. He observed that, apart from contact with children, the life back home seemed a world away. He enjoyed the headspace that solo cycling provides and the consuming demands of getting from A to B didn't allow for many home thoughts from abroad.

5
THE MOTHERSHIP RETURNS
AND THE FINES ARE TOTTED UP

While Dowdeswells and Sorensens enjoyed an extra couple of days relaxing in Istanbul, the Mothership was repatriated by her mummy and daddy.

In Clive's words:

> The journey home - was scheduled to be a lovely, gentle journey back to The Hook of Holland and England over 11 days. Karen who, with the other ladies, had joined us in Istanbul was so very, very understanding. The fact was that, for me, it was all a bit 'After The Lord Mayor's Show.' I was elated to have achieved what we had achieved and the journey back was, to be honest, an inconvenience to be got out of the way. On top of that, the weather on the way back was as wet as it had been dry throughout our cycle.
>
> I was therefore really grateful to Karen when she gave up her idea of a meandering tour of Europe and replaced it with a 'Motorways of Europe' trip. Given that we covered around 2400 miles in 7 days, the Mothership did a magnificent job in averaging 350 miles a day - 6 or more hours of driving every day. A combination of known and new hotels, and favoured campsites in Germany and Holland saw us back to The Hook of Holland a week early. Luckily we were able to amend our ticket and we happily found ourselves back in England undertaking the rigours of the Monday morning rush-hour. Strangely, never has it had such a welcoming feel.

By the time we reached Istanbul we had raised over £5000, which rose to nearly £7000 by the time Clive closed the Just Giving page at the end of October. It's hard to calculate how much the trip cost each of us. We paid for it in dribs and drabs, piecemeal as the expenses occurred. I guess around £2000 each. Not bad for a month's physical purgatory!

At the end Chris's spreadsheet equalised the expenditure of our little black book but the final reckoning may be yet to come. The

Mothership's misdemeanours seem, regularly, to come back to haunt us. I asked Clive to give a rundown of the damage so far.

Unbeknownst to us, the fines started a few weeks before we had even set out. I had no idea that the Mothership would be subject to London's 'Low Emission Zone' so the original transgression was on a visit to Paul and Belinda's before a training session in Richmond Park. It was only when receiving a WhatsApp message from Karen, at the Berger Campsite in Germany, that the first indication of a problem emerged. Suffice it to say that we soon realised that we had erred again when we set off from the London Eye on the 15th September. Ugh! £300 down. Later on that same day, whilst looking for a seemingly lost Paul in darkest Essex, Chris and I crossed into a 'Buses only' zone...er...twice. £60 which I am grateful to report was cancelled by the friendly Essex County Council when they took pity on us either because of the good cause or because of the utter incompetence of it all. London Mayor, Sadiq Khan had no such scruples despite my letter of appeal (which incidentally used those two reasons as a method of defence -1. A good cause, BeatSCAD, and 2. We are incompetents).

Once on the continent, we felt all would be well and were intrigued by the 'Viagem' signs along many of the major roads and motorways. 'Must be tourist routes,' I ventured. It was only on the way home when stopped and fined 80 Lev in Bulgaria (around £40) that I realised that these were permits which needed to be bought to use the roads - oops! Actually, we'd been lucky because we had never bought these daily permits and arrived in Istanbul unscathed financially, in that respect anyway. I made up for that on the way back; charged for motorway use in Turkey, fined in Bulgaria, photographed and later fined in Hungary for lack of 'Viagem.' That final fine of £64 arrived three months later via a Surrey-based debt collection company.

We also had a couple of parking issues. Parking ticket outside the hostel in Backa Palanka, Serbia and a parking ticket for parking illegally in a Vienna car park (no motorhomes apparently). In both instances we took the advice of a friendly Austrian hotelier, 'If it's from the government, pay. If it's from a private company, ignore.' We ignored and thus far have heard no more.

This could be famous last words but we're all past caring.

EPILOGUE AND ACKNOWLEDGEMENTS

I first drafted this epilogue on July 10th, the day of Vera Lynn's funeral. What a life she has led and what an inspiration she was to the nation in dark times then...and now. One of the mantras that I have heard far too often is that 'Life ain't no rehearsal'. The implication is that we should always be in search of the extraordinary. What I have learned is to enjoy the extraordinary pleasure of the everyday. The real enjoyment of our Eye to I was just that: a daily bike ride taking in the surroundings, good chatter with friends, a hot shower and a cold beer.

It is October 15th. Liverpool is in lockdown and our government is squirming ever more embarrassingly as the second wave of Covid reaches crisis levels. To make matters worse, Harry McGuire got sent off last night as England succumbed to the power of mighty Denmark at Wembley. My Dad would be clapping in his grave. These final thoughts will be sent to Andrew Sparke, my publisher who deserves my great thanks for his work and skill in helping me see this project through. Thanks too, to my friend and brilliant cartoonist, Dave Chisholm, who has fashioned a wonderful illustration of our journey for the opening pages.

It is just a year since we returned from Istanbul, but what a strange time it has been. Much has been said and written about the change in our world in such a short time. There is more to come as we search for answers and seek to recover from mistakes. Many thousands are bereaved. A recalibrating of priorities and an acceptance of our common humanity are badly needed.

My greatest thanks, of course go to my partners in crime, Clive and Chris. Thanks for the memories and for helping me plug those gaps where my memory was bettered by yours. A group hug for our ladies, Belinda, Sarah and Karen. Each made a singular and special contribution. To those working for BeatSCAD and those who have suffered with it, we hope that our efforts made a small difference. Thanks to all our friends and family and even our old school who contributed so generously. Thanks, too, to those who followed our exploits on Facebook and websites, giving cheeky encouragement all the way.

Our Eye2i challenge was Clive Rockell's brainchild. Two old school mates, literally went along with him for the ride. We are very glad that we did.

MEMOIRS & LOCAL HISTORY FROM APS BOOKS
www.andrewsparke.com

Beating The Banana: Breast Cancer and Me (Helen Pitt)
Bella In The Wych-Elm (Andrew Sparke)
Countdown Cath (Cathy Hytner)
Croc Curry & Texas Tea: Surviving Nigeria (Paul Dickinson)
Istanbul: The Visitor Essentials (Andrew Sparke)
Leaving Lewis (Helen Pitt)
Magna Carta Wars Of Lincoln Cathedral (Andrew Sparke)
More Swings Than Roundabouts (John Wright)
Piggery Jokery In Tonga (Andrew Sparke)
Rear Gunner (Andrew Sparke)
Tales From Pinfold Farm (Helen Pitt)
The Erstwhile Buddhist (Helen Pitt)
The Strange Free-Fall Of Fred Ryland (Helen Pitt)
The Ways Of Mevagissey (Andrew Sparke)
What I Think About When I Think about Aikido (Mark Peckett)
Who Put Bella In The Wych Elm? The Crime Scene Revisited (Alex Merrill)

Printed in Poland
by Amazon Fulfillment
Poland Sp. z o.o., Wrocław

63706040R00078